AGENDA

CONTENTS

Editorial   3

POEMS

Andrew Waterman: *In the Hereafter*   5
           After that Winter   6
Tim Dooley: *Song*   7
     The Old Ones   7
Marc Harris: *Watered Tomatoes*   8
     River Dreams   8
Linda Saunders: *Hide and Seek*   9
     Playing Alone   9
     Paleontologist   10
Darius Degher: *Watershed*   11
Lenny Emmanuel: *After the Storm*   12
Steven Knauth: *Breeze Bringing Dusk*   13
     Fighter Pilot   14
Sally Carr: *My Father's Music Cabinet*   15
     The Weight of Petals   16
Peter Robinson: *Ratifying Kyoto*   17
Alison Brackenbury: *The Girls of the Pietà*   18
Alex Small: *Shiva's Dance*   19
     Time Team   19
David Cooke: *Benares*   20
Marianne Burton: *Changing the Sheets*   21
     August Break: Bournemouth Sands   22
W.S. Milne: *Your Garden Narcissi*   23
Robert Sheppard: *Poem*   24
Mark Leech: *Bird Hits Glass*   25
     Sonnet (Lorca)   25

ESSAYS/REVIEWS

Martin Dodsworth: The God of Details: translations and adaptations
     of Ted Hughes and Derek Mahon   26
William Bedford: Observation Transformed Into Vision:Ted Hughes: A
     Literary Life by Neil Roberts   40

TWO POEMS

Annie Charlesworth: A Letter to the Dead
(for Ted Hughes and Sylvia Plath) 48
William Bedford: Cold Stars 52

W.S.Milne: A Standing-Stone: Michael Longley's *Collected Poems* 53
Patricia McCarthy: A Question of Androgyny: Eavan Boland and
Fiona Sampson 57
Kate Edwards: chosen young Broadsheet essayist:
The Revolving Epoch: David Jones and Oswald Spengler 68

POEMS

Harriet Torr: The Old Soldier 75
Sally Lucas: Seven Chakras 76

TRANSLATIONS/VERSIONS

Boris Poplavsky: White Halo: **Belinda Cooke** 80
Untitled: **Richard McKane** 80
Boris Pasternak: Mushrooming: **Belinda Cooke** 82
Superstition: **Richard McKane** 83

TWO CHOSEN YOUNG BROADSHEET POETS

Julie Barraclough: A Lost Journey 84
Michael Molan: Fragment 87
Penelope in London; in London; as a
twenty-three-year-old man 87
Cristo Deposto 88
Milan 89

Notes for Broadsheet Poets 9 90

Interview: Peter Robinson interviewed by Belinda Cooke 91

Biographies 95

Thomas Hardy Society Poetry Competition 97

Editorial

Welcome again to another *Agenda*, this time a single issue that you can slip into your pocket or bag and dip into on the train, bus or wherever. The overall theme was meant to be a different one. However, as is often the case with *Agenda*, something happens at the last minute to make the issue gel in an unforeseen way. This is sometimes due to the constraints regarding the number of pages. Nevertheless a magic often occurs. The Muse intervening? William Cookson, the founding editor up, above – who always went by instinct? Who knows?

Whatever. What binds this issue, as it happens, in the essays/reviews, is the theme of the past defined articulately in the piece by Kate Edwards, **chosen young Broadsheet essayist**, on David Jones (last in the essays), who has long been associated with *Agenda*. In fact, William Cookson knew him well. He had many a cup of tea with the man and promoted his work out of a profound belief in it (see past issues of *Agenda*: David Jones Special issue Vol 5, Nos 1-3, Spring/summer 1967, and another David Jones Special issue Vol.11 No.4/Vol.12 No.1 Autumn/winter 1973/4, as well as other issues of the journal. Prose works published by **Agenda Editions** – still available – include David Jones: *The Roman Quarry*, edited by Harman Grisewood and René Hague, 284 pages, £13.50 including postage; David Jones' *Letters to William Hayward*, edited by Colin Wilcockson, 80 pages, £11 including postage; and *The Kensington Mass*, the unfinished draft of a poem which David Jones started to write in 1973 and was working on at the time of his death, £7 including postage).

The past, then, begins with what makes David Jones different from the other poets of the Great War. The answer: seemingly in his approach not only to the parallel, as he saw it, of art to war, but also to time (something akin to the eternally recurring present, maybe, as J.B. Priestley conceived it, or to Eliot's 'timeless moments'), to history and its repeated patterns, to translators of poetic works of yore, to memory and our own pasts, and to our ways of coping with it all. Essays/reviews of Ted Hughes's and Derek Mahon's translations, including those of the classics; of Hughes' own work, especially that of *Birthday Letters* which revolves around his personal 'wars' in his marriage to Sylvia Plath, depending on how they are viewed; of Michael Longley's corpus of poetry, including his writings on the Great War, and on the 'Troubles' in his own native Northern Ireland; Eavan Boland's perspective on Irish history as a 'woman poet'; and Fiona Sampson's invocation of the present, with its inherent near pasts and immanent futures.

Of course, it could be argued that all art, including poetry, is a recording, and, as such, a part of the past, since the present vanishes as soon as it is named.

The poems in this issue pertain to anything and everything, as all poetry should; except for a couple of poems addressed specifically to Hughes and Plath, one a 'Letter' which, along with Ted Hughes' *Birthday Letters*, recalls the actual correspondence exchanged between Ted Hughes and William Cookson, founding Editor, over a number of years, as well as some very early work of Ted Hughes included in early issues of *Agenda*. There is also a soothing sequence of Chakras to help the hard-pressed amongst us.

The **chosen Broadsheet poets** in this issue, and the chosen **Broadsheet poets online** (along with chosen young artists) make most of us feel not only very humble, but that there is a huge future for poetry while humanity prevails.

Do visit **the website** www.agendapoetry.co.uk to read these Broadsheets for young poets and young artists. Also look at the poems and paintings in the online general supplements, and translations, as well as the online essays. The carefully selected contents are of a very high standard, equal to the work displayed in the magazine. The website is gaining more and more prominence as an international showcase for and supplement to *Agenda*.

Many thanks to everyone associated with *Agenda*. Please make sure you keep up to date with your subscriptions, as we rely on our subscribers for the flourishing of the magazine. If you have submitted work, and have not yet heard back from us, please be patient as we have a huge backlog, and we will be getting back to you.

It is hoped that every subscriber, buyer and contributor to *Agenda* will enjoy this issue, along with all the others, and will find inspiration and sustenance in its pages.

Patricia McCarthy, Editor
Marcus Frederick, Administrator

The next Ted Hughes conference will be held at Pembroke College, Cambridge, on 16-18 September, 2012. Enquiries to t.gifford@chi.ad.uk

---

Agenda wishes to pay tribute to a regular and long-time contributor, the well-known poet, translator and essayist, **Michael Hamburger**, 1924-2007, who died on June 7th, 2007.
Agenda hopes, in future issues, to honour Michael with retrospective essays and memoirs.

Andrew Waterman

In the Hereafter

Forget eternity, give me just one day.
The big white house above a scoop of sea,
whin spilling gold down glen behind it.
They've all turned up… Some, fresh from a dawn swim
are mooching round the garden, its great trees,
gazebo, flowerbeds where no petal drops;
but most, back late last night from the pub
where the fiddler brought down the rafters, are inside
sipping coffees. There are no hangovers.
Dogs barking, cock-crows from a distant field,
the high whirr of a coastguard helicopter
 confirm all's true, with the sun's heat
in fissured stones of this wall I lean upon.

Letting things be. So they play chess, or tennis
(swift as my thought, the courts appear),
devour the afternoon light with passionate talk.
A kindling, astonishingly become
the blaze life dreams of, nothing out of place
but, as it should be perpetually surprising.

When evening brings all indoors, there's the party.
For you, my friends from scattered years and places,
not least those I lost track of through neglects,
sad fallings-out, or time's attrition.
Effaced among the throng, my satisfaction
is seeing how, at what for most's first meeting,
you like each other. As the moon sails out
from a hill, I slip away, to leave you talking:
books, love, jokes, blood fired, our music playing.

After That Winter

With the equinox, a spring of sorts,
snow-melt and the river flowing fuller,
after the worst of bitter winters, when
the Spirits had neglected to protect them,
no elk herd came to spear, when the last child
died just three of them were left from thirty,
the two men gut-sick and the grieving mother.
They reasoned it out, and left their place, and headed
towards where daily the sun reached its zenith,
veering only to keep nearby to water.
On the twelfth day they chanced on an encampment,
strange tongues weighed their wary overtures,
then let them stay and work. Until the cold
came back, then wanted just to keep the woman.
They left the place.
                              And walked, as you could then,
so much of water being locked-up in ice
they'd never strayed enough to grasp the scale of,
across a low plain, aiming at the sun.
Weaker than sabre-tooth, they used their wits,
fashioning flints, and snares of twig and thong,
and never quite taken in by those they encountered
heard at last rumours of a fabled warm land,
its glut to hunt and pluck: 'Beyond those mountains.'
Stopping them in their tracks with mighty ice-fangs.
Against all reason. She was with child again,
they found a place. Enough to be going on with.

For twenty thousand years. Until, the miles-deep
ridged mass gargling boulders in its melt-mush
having conceded passage, over the Alps
spread villas, vineyards. Leaping where now sea was
to march straight roads right up to where they'd started.
Blank to its reason's outcomes: pushbutton slaughter,
myself here conjuring Mozart from a disc.
Cradled with *Pax Romana* and our fetid
puff of cataclysmic global warming
in a brief intermission, before Earth's next
orbital wobble brings the glaciers back.

Tim Dooley

Song

I passed the warning signs.
My skin was scratched with briars.
I found the hidden lake
where the heron's wing caught fire.

My skin was scratched with briars.
My cuffs were grey and torn.
Where the heron's wing caught fire
I was suddenly transformed.

The surface glistened red and green
beyond the boundary wire
as if a sparkling stone
nestled in my palm.

Beyond the boundary wire,
I found the hidden lake
nestling, in my palm,
beyond the warning signs.

The Old Ones

after Horace *Odes* I xi

Don't ask. No-one can tell me or tell you,
Lucky, that it's time to go. Don't throw
the I Ching, or dice, or lay out Tarot cards.
Don't – it's beneath you – check your horoscope.
Whatever happens you'll put up with it.
That's best. Let's not ask if this is the last time
that we'll watch the sea off Walberswick
eroding the land, waves by gasping waves.

Gather your sloes and bottle them in gin.
Prune back the stems of your high hopes to the
space that's left. While we talk, the hours gather
to take flight. Don't go South with them. Carve out
what you can. Tomorrow no-one will credit
how little you've left to be missed or mourned.

7

Marc Harris

Watered Tomatoes

He used to treat them like children,
his Wenallt tomatoes.
He'd strain sheep manure,
lovingly gathered
from the damp mountainside
in old Hessian sacks
in a tin bath
flush with rainwater.

And the tomatoes,
the sweetest I'd ever tasted,
would sip the brown liquid
from the soft soil
like sugared tea.

Wenallt is the Welsh word for *fair hillside* or *wood*.

River Dreams

Spun
in a weed-strewn moon's reflecton;
recollections –
where coracles swirled in salmon pools
on Tywi, Teifi, Taff;
of Dai the ferryman,
rock for a pillow –
sound asleep.

Where otters creep
willows weep shade into water canvas –
brush of feather-blue,
crush of lovers' limbs –
cool summer pools.

In the dew
spirits' feet;
two tides meet,
'Croeso I Gymru' –
'Welcome to Wales'.

Linda Saunders

Hide and Seek

The perfect place – so narrow only she,
the smallest and youngest, could thread
herself in, slung like a secret drawer
in the oaken underbelly of the dresser,
suspended in woody twilight.

A cloak of darkness was always
the fairy's gift she longed for,
a slim purse from which to unfold
her vanishing, a weave almost immaterial
baffling light like the mirror skin of water.

*

Surely she's been waiting most of a lifetime
to slip through the stuff of the given,
be lost, and come up elsewhere.
Listening at the crack between words
and their meaning, becoming wood but also

air,
testing her own absence
in the quiet room, drifting out
beyond the walls, while the others
are still moving around the house calling 'Coming'.

Playing Alone

I'd turn up the mirror on my mother's table,
where it lay among trinkets, tortoiseshell combs,
boxes of talc, Pond's vanishing cream,

always face down – to stop you falling
in its echoing well, or cover a gaze
that sees too much when you're not watching.

Then I'd lift it just below my eyes to look
along the surface like a swimmer, and down
into a stark geometry that would rock

and lean as I tacked across white plains
of ceiling, only edges and corners for bearings,
or a light sprouting straight up like a tulip.

Eyes-down, I drifted in the upside
otherworld; fording soft shadows
and shifty refractions; high-stepping

low walls of lintels into courts of illusion.
My feet, lost in the deep rugs of reason,
stubbed toes on intractable ghosts.

Returning, I sensed a difference, strange
stillness of things, biding their ground with such
cunning, chairs and vases colluding

in the grown-up game; her flask of cologne,
crystal swan, myself in a silver frame
near the mirror I'd replaced – anchored

through habit and a stolid gravity,
letting us believe life is the right way up
and, for the time being, safe.

Paleontologist

Coaxes from sand
tight bud of a knuckle, the knee's curious petal,
femur and fibula, the articulate sacrum,
cleansing and counting carpal
and metacarpal, saying
the beads of the body.
Cradles at last like a newborn
the occiput in her palm,
blows light
into the dark sockets of the eyes.

Darius Degher

Watershed

You'll see both rivers from that watershed.
And though it's understandable to cling
turn gently to the one that lies ahead.

Even if the edges of an umbra spread
and you worry over flocks scattering
you'll see both rivers from that watershed.

Although you will have gathered words unsaid
and unsung love sighing and blustering
look gently to the one that lies ahead.

Though you know well the frame is limited
you'll wish another spring were issuing.
Accept both rivers from that watershed.

Of course you're bound to be unsure, misled
by science and religion wondering.
Turn gently to the one that lies ahead.

Perhaps there are no images to dread,
no forests of darkness and reckoning.
You'll see both rivers from that watershed.
Go gently to the one that lies ahead.

Lenny Emmanuel

After The Storm

The postman says
he will discontinue the mail
if the tree limbs are not cut.

After the storm,
gladiolas and morning glories
cling to a dying oak.

Sparrows and seagulls
feed on crumbs
leftover by drunken seamen.

The ocean liner
is still moving slowly across
the bleak horizon.

Without saying goodbye,
the slim girl is still
swimming and swimming.

Pages of old books
turn with their marginal marks,
searching for answers.

Here on Tybee Island
tangled grape vines strangle
maples and willows.

The channel markers
and beacons are all gone,
but this salty seawall remains.

The broken screens
of these beach house windows
survive the malcontent sea.

Lean white hounds wait
near old railroad tracks
for the lights beyond the darks.

Fog horns sound up
and down the Savannah River
through the damp, dark nights.

If you ever come back,
don't try to revive the willows.
We *could*... plant a few small palms.

Stephen Knauth

Breeze Bringing Dusk

Shyly the leaves show their private side.
Chaste silver of an alpine moon. Don't look
too long. Something about turning away
then back freshens desire, like leaving home
and returning thirty years later, same lawn,
different boy pushing the mower. Desire
for what, desire itself? The old aunties knew
how to slip away without dying – nothing
special, *digesting*, they were, *resting*.
Placing a hand on theirs was a queer
transfusion we'd not understood.
Resting, while the rest of us watched *Bonanza*.
Their skin, cosmology of faint objects
glimpsed again last night, *mine*, reaching for the lamp –
what else did we miss back then?
The fairy story about the sad giant,
asleep in the forest, cradling his withered twin.
We listened, drifted off on a breeze
from the sea. Yesterday and tomorrow,
looking for a way to pass between them.
Shyly the lindens show us the tender rend.

Fighter Pilot

I'm chewing Dad's gum tonight
the last piece from the last pack
he left on the bedside table.
Peppermint Dentyne Ice
it reminds me of him
how I'd inhale sharply
when he entered the room
after his fourth or fifth drink
or when he'd call on the phone
on those necessary occasions
voice low and fixed
delivering bad news.
The last time I saw him
he'd grown pale and gaunt
harsh features emerging like a skyline at dusk.
We sat together in that swaddled room
and watched the shuttle go up from the Cape.
He didn't say much, staring
straight ahead at the screen the whole time.
He seemed to be concentrating
as if he was flying the damn thing himself.
I'll say this, he was calm and cool
at the controls that day, clear-eyed,
steady rhythm of his grizzled jaw,
until all we saw was a tiny amber stain of light.

Sally Carr

My Father's Music Cabinet

Then there were all the dreamt-of pieces,
Chopin Nocturnes, Impromptus, Études;
annotated by him in that assertive hand,
capable of a drumming percussion
that transformed the house, echoed out
into the garden on summer evenings.
As a child, I'd dance in my pyjamas,
prance and leap, point skinny feet.
His name, though faded in blue-black ink,
is still emphatic on the covers, with dates
as old as '48, even '38 … and I think
what a serious young man, playing
to please his friends in the Fraternity House
in the depths of ice and snow in Iowa,
far from difficult Belfast, his mother,
and the source of Protestant work-demons …
In my battered Beethoven book, a school prize,
there are palimpsests: of *his* writing alongside,
above, or even contradicting
my teacher's instructions, where he'd gone back
to much simpler stuff, such as *Für Elise,*
when the arthritis really began to claw …
I should find a new home for all of this.
But not yet, not while just opening a drawer
makes the room reverberate, like a first chord
on that black Bechstein grand, that dwarfed
the armchairs in our suburban sitting room,
and which I somehow knew even then,
along with his other flamboyant acquisitions,
we couldn't really afford. Yet the genie
of the music's out … and that big, warm laugh …
together, they fill to a *crescendo.*

The Weight of Petals

who could paint precisely
this velvet-maroon?
a fragrance to climb inside

yet feather-petals on the palm
no more than a breath -
while in my head a naming psalm

Tuscany Ispahan Belle de Crecy
Autumn Damask
Paul's Himalayan Musk

I'd grow them all,
walk amongst them at dusk
in their celestial cloister

brushing nap of newborn's cheek
satin of lips I've kissed
brocade of scarce-touched fingertips –

soon they'll drift to the path
slow flutter of the Lovely
too numerous to be counted

Peter Robinson

Ratifying Kyoto

In a transitory light, you see
low sun's throwing elongated shadows
of branches, wires, telephone poles;
it's casting them across snow remnants
or a house wall's second storey
where your own, entangled with them,
(as if you were that shadow cast)
tells of only chill deferrals —
no end of them at a winter's end.

It's one of those underprivileged moments
when the protocols of snow
are pushed aside to exhaust neglect,
when, talk notwithstanding, some holes
are poked in the sky, in the sky
and in our arguments.

So you ratify Kyoto
criss-crossing the city in search of traces
where each grief and trauma
came to be expressed: you're here
to find a future habitat, a home, or
roof above our heads at least; the space is
still sadder, no wiser and you,
you haven't a pallid idea.

Alison Brackenbury

The girls of the Pietà

They were the daughters of the street
Or its granddaughters. Money met
A hot hand; though the chime was brief
One spasm stopped thick blood's relief.
Its rhythms drowned by muscles' ache
The soundless kick, the low dress strained,
The clients cut off like a song.
The red-face bundle dumped upon
The doorstep of the Pietà,

Which, in the end, sunk to the way
Of Venice, with the girls turned whore.
But in its prime, trained voices soared
In monthly concert, ringless hands
Grasped the viola's varnished band
Musicians, oddly, called 'the soul'.
With artless hair, they stood in rows
Each starch-stiff bodice whiter than
The watery couplings of the sun
On their scrubbed floor. Their music's flood
Washed round the seated; velvet hoods,
Boots tight on strong calves. All were still.
Breath, by those sounds and stone floors, chilled.

The concert ended. Freed to night's
Warm tide, pairs walked, hands clasping light.
One, as the girls packed music sheets,
In silence sought the dark wet streets.

Alexander Small

How All Iterates Shiva's Dance

That nothingness the all's hung on
forms its forever from what has gone,
what is, and – as the all implies –
a someday's symmetries devise:

vast age out of vaster rages torn,
from the screaming silence stars are born
its flowerings, that themselves deflower,
each sullen seeding spawning power

to darken darkness, nulling night,
that light – a daintier appetite –
consume as cause what coughs the core
certainty's still searching for.

So darkly spins this lightsome dance
in two-step, all steps done by chance:
real-time's reeling never halts…
But when's it my dance? Where's my waltz?

Time Team

That the fading be stilled, seem held in trust,
his final weight, what the wind`s hand
thrust is story, writ in sand...
sometime stirring from an empty cast.

The echo's long, whose long lost son
time sepulchred a blackening stone...
peeled, warm flesh conforms the bone.

David Cooke

Benares

He pleased a woman and a woman pressed
Her mind against him until he ceased
To dream and woke and again confessed.

Money borrowed but a year's return.
Benares he cuts the cards until
The living creatures flame and burn.

From ash he rises with the dust
To flame above their pyre until
Once again they enact their lust.

He pleased a woman and a woman said:
He moves about and the dark does sleep
And curl its dream around his head.

Beauty crumbled while their demands
Broke a year – their cards were dressed by
Benares who watched with naked hands.

Such stock returned but a year's supply.
The roots of us go down the deep, only
Benares moves about and does not die,
But rises as the dream is said.

Marianne Burton

Changing The Sheets

Nothing more intimate
than this tending.
Though these are not
special, not wedding

sheets, no child
was born in them.
They have no rolled
hand-sewn hems,

are not embroidered
with sprigs of gorse.
Not new, not ironed.
Just creased, coarse,

cheap store cotton
for the Arundel tomb
where we clutch. Twins
in our night womb.

Not perfumed, not linen.
Just your sleep sweat,
acid and a peck of salt,
safe in my keeping.

August Break : Bournemouth Sands

He was all curves,
hunchback chin nose,
sharp as sabre blades.

Mr. Supreme Arrogance,
red-hot in velvet, slinging his legs
over the striped awning as he crowed

and fed into his mincer
the Black Man for black sausages,
the Policeman for black and white, black and white.

He wielded his baton
over us – threepence on the seawall,
sixpence for the gritty carpet in front of the booth

with free colouring card
or custard cream, the breeze inflating
our cardigans like windsocks – and we cheered

and laughed
as Judy was coshed to death,
the baby tossed and dropped until its skull broke

and the sands grew rosy
in the glow of Grand Guignol.
No one told him off for wetting the bed a second night.

And although the crocodile,
limbless and wordless, instrument of the furies,
always proved more powerful, we remained his puppets,

hand in glove,
walking home to High Tea down the Esplanade,
where fathers mothers and babies waited in small dark hotel rooms.

W.S. Milne

Your Garden Narcissi

You are tending them: such flowers
As are given to us freely
As gifts almost to handsel and cherish
And give in return. As the earth
Comes to life again, you scutter
And potter about in our garden,
And the starlings – beyond the dyke –
Throng the fields, hungry, forsaken.
Melt-water runs, the sun blinks off ice
(There is a sheet of ice mantling the pond).
There is a simple dream of peace here,
Almost to walk through the soul's labyrinth,
Far from the world's crabbed ways.
Spring's gentle fire burns in these flowers
You tend, enough to make the heart speak out,
And make the words stand for light.
The apple-blossom too gems and buds,
Giving hope to the derelict and desolate soul.
The earth is at its making. Love guards us well.
The poet's pact with words, his passion,
Is like this too: bluebells rapt in transience,
Heirs of the passing day, its spell, its trance,
Avid for love's ways, its passion.
Our tree sways and dances. You see me and wave
(You are tugging at a thistle clutching the clay)
And I think: what is best for this age
Is probably the broken sentence,
But these words, I hope, beguile the day.

Robert Sheppard

Poem

The unmistaken girl and her
Shapely back take the

Poem, lift it off your tongue.
She passes and it pursues her

Brown shoulders shrugging
And the deep gorge of flesh

Stretching down her spine.
Desiring her sun-sheened

Back the poem waits; the lazy
Sky paints blank blue

Unhazed. At the kerb
Where she dances, her

Shadow shaves across a white
Sheet of street trash

Dazzling like blank
Paper. It stirs in starting

Breeze, rattles over cobbles,
Flips on its back, waits

To be tickled like a
Beast, or fed with her eyes.

The girl knows the part
She plays in this trick: a walk-on

In a poem about nothing
Much. She won't turn back.

She absorbs the poem like heat. It
Becomes her, she becomes

Its loss, its distance, turning cool
Into echo under the railway bridge,

A shadow, unscheduled,
Without a thing to throw it.

The accidental woman with the perfect
shoulders steals the poem
from my lips. She strolls past

and the poem follows her dark
rolling shoulder-blades and the long
hollow that enfleshes her flexing spine.

The poem wants her for its own.
The sun shines fierce, the sky
yawns deep blue unflecked with

white. In the gutter where her sharp
shadow sways, a discarded
square of hardboard, as blinding white

as the sheet of un-
written-upon paper before me now,
shivers in some freak gust,

slithers across the stones loose in
melting tarmac, clatters for her
to twist her body round. Yet she won't.

The young woman knows she is
but sun-glinted back glimpsed once in
a poem about something else

and refuses to turn. The poem she spirits
away round the corner, out of eyeshot,
tunnelled into shadow;

an echo of its unformer self.

Mark Leech

Bird Hits Glass

Artificial flower furious in panic,
the flat *whack* of the strike still trembles it.
               My bare feet dust across the patio:
               uncertain rescue stoops.

Soft, then cracker brittle in the hand,
the heart another finger tapping code.

               The beak jolts at me, the gaudy
               crucifixion writhes hot animal,
rejects my palms' merciful cup:
flick, flight, danger call.

Sonnet

(from the Spanish by Federico Garcia Lorca)

Long-tailed spectre of shifting silver,
the night wind, stretching, sighing,
reopened my old hurt with grey fingers
and left: I went back to my desiring.

Wound of love that gave me life,
eternal spring of pure light gushing,
crevice in which mute Philomena finds
her nest, forest, grief, all blooming.

How sweetness gabbles in my head!
I'll lie beside the simple flower
where your unsouled beauty's fled
and roaming water yellows;
my blood seeps through marshes, down
to the fragrant rushes on the coast.

Martin Dodsworth

The God of Details

Ted Hughes, *Selected Translations*, edited by Daniel Weissbort, Faber, £20.00

Derek Mahon, *Adaptations*, Gallery Press, Ireland, €18.50 hb, £12.95 pb

Reading translations of poetry which have been made by poets tests the reader, because a double work of interpretation is required. You must try to understand both what the translator has done and what of the original is refracted through its new language. The reward, though, is also double, a double pleasure accruing when we feel we truly grasp the sense of a translation. For that to happen, there first has to be the effort of understanding, and, indeed, judging; not all readers or poets welcome such an emphasis on judgement. Yet judgement is given a prominent part in the history of translation. It figures significantly in one of the earliest accounts in English, Roscommon's *Essay on Translated Verse* (1684): 'good *Translation* is no *easie* Art ... by *Improving* what was writ *Before,/ Invention* Labours *Less*, but *Judgment more*'. So it should be. We may not nowadays seek to 'improve' on the original, but even to equal it requires more than a screwing-up of courage and a stab in the dark. And as to the exercise of judgement Roscommon's advice to the translator goes straight to the point:

> The first great work (a Task perform'd by few)
> *Is* that *your self* may to *your self* be true:
> No *Masque*, no *Tricks*, no *Favour*, no *Reserve*;
> *Dissect* your Mind, examine ev'ry *Nerve*.
> Whoever *Vainly* on his *strength* depends,
> *Begins* like *Virgil*, but like *Maevius Ends* ...

The difference between Ted Hughes and Derek Mahon as translators lies in the degree to which each of them exercises his judgement. Whether either of them 'improves' on his original will reflect the use to which judgement is put.

Translation undoubtedly played an important part in Ted Hughes's creative life, and Daniel Weissbort, his friend and co-founder with him of *Modern Poetry in Translation*, has put together a book intended to illustrate this. 'The achievement of Ted Hughes as a poet is inseparable from his achievement as a translator of poetry and poetic drama,' we are told on the jacket of the handsome *Selected Translations*; in his introduction Weissbort claims that Hughes 'was among the most important poetry translators in the English tradition.' This is talking big, and many readers will wonder what there is to back it up. On the face of it, Hughes's commitment to a form of mid-twentieth-century primitivism would make him uninterested in the kind of self-examination advocated by Roscommon, and this would, in turn, limit the scrupulosity of his response to the work of others. The major authors translated by Hughes were Aeschylus, Euripides, Racine and Lorca.

He also tackled a large part of the *Metamorphoses*. The versions of Ovid had great success when they came out, but the others, also end-of-career work, had a quiet reception. Something more than assertion is needed, then, to establish their achievement. Unfortunately, Weissbort is unable to supply it.

This is partly because he is reluctant to think beyond Hughes's own view of translation, that 'the first ideal is literalness', a view formulated in the sixties and reiterated in the eighties. Writing on his own behalf and that of Weissbort in 1982 of their work for *MPT*, he observed:

> Since our only real motive in publishing was our own curiosity in contemporary foreign poetry, we favoured the translations that best revealed the individuality and strangeness of the original. This usually meant a translation that interposed the minimum of the reflexes and inventions of the translator.

Throughout the *Selected Translations* Weissbort pushes the idea of 'literalness' as Hughes's ideal, and, indeed, as an ideal in translation altogether. Perhaps this is because he himself favoured 'literalness' as a criterion for the work published in *MPT*. But 'literalness' in translation, though often called for (there has been correspondence on the subject this year in the *TLS*), is not the uncomplicated thing it represents itself to be. Hughes thinks of it in terms of repressing 'the reflexes and inventions of the translator', as though it were merely a matter of removing personal quirks. But word-for-word 'literalness' is an impossibility, because there is no exact calibration between languages. English, for example, has grammatical forms that are lacking in French, and *vice versa*. The two languages share many concepts but not all, and they bear the impress of different histories. These truths may be generalized to all languages. If Hughes was able to overlook them it was because he tended to look through words to a 'universal' grammar of myth underlying poetry. Among his many, often helpful appendices, Weissbort gives us Hughes's programme note for the Poetry International '67, in which he writes of poetry as 'a Universal language of understanding, coherent behind the many languages in which we can all hope to meet'. The invented language of *Orghast*, of which Weissbort gives us a morsel (though it is hardly translation) plainly relates to this idea of the 'Universal' language. Hughes described it as 'stripping off the intrusive, formal, merely communicative or intercommunicative element of language – that intellectual and loaded side of language'.

Hughes's praise of 'literalism' is part of the anti-intellectualism of his poetic practice (and his dismissal of what is 'communicative or intercommunicative' offers one explanation for the slack and repetitive side of his later poems). But 'literalism' served the writers of *MPT*'s early years well. Poets like Popa and Holub, or Pilinszky whom Hughes himself translated, wrote in opposition to the official state ideology and its language. Their poetry is couched in terms that rebuke the mendacious intellectualism and internationalism which dominated the world in which they wrote. British and American readers probably missed, and continue to miss, much that is culturally specific in the poetry of (for example) Popa, but his anti-intellectualism, his frankness about suffering and his fascination with legend, whether of the nursery or the people, were well served in the English of Anne Pennington. Similarly, Hughes's versions of Pilinszky successfully conveyed what the poet himself called the 'linguistic poverty' of his poetry. They were based on rough drafts provided by someone who understood the original Hungarian, Janos Csokits; 'very many lines of his ... have been impossible to improve as far as I could judge,' wrote Hughes. The fact that Hughes felt that he could nevertheless, and in ignorance of the poems' original language, 'improve' on the rough drafts to some degree clearly indicates that 'literalism' for him is not quite what literalism might be for other people. Weissbort prints two stanzas from Csokits's drafts which show that, although Hughes was happy to retain some phrases outright, others were, as might be expected, decisively made over by him. Here are the last lines of 'The French Prisoner' version:

He who would have subsisted on any aliment:
is demanding now my heart.

Hughes changed this to:

And now he, who would have eaten anything,
is clamouring for my heart.

Which is the more literal? Do 'subsisted' and 'aliment' reflect something in the Hungarian that Hughes misses? Those of us without Hungarian cannot tell. Hughes's greater simplicity and directness in the first line are convincing, just as the raised stakes of 'clamouring' for 'demanding' in the second one convince, but the disappearance of 'aliment' and the relocation of 'now' certainly look like sins against 'literalism', literally interpreted. May they not be reflexes and inventions of the translator, such as Hughes himself decried? You might say that to argue thus is to argue too curiously, but the point of 'literalism' must be that details matter. Given the impossibility of absolute literalism, the translator is under an obligation to decide which details matter most. That is why judgement matters. In modifying Csokits, Hughes used his judgement, despite his commitment to 'literalism', and we cannot but be grateful.

Hughes's opposition to the 'intellectual and loaded' side of language made it difficult for him to use his judgement in translation as he should have. Certainly, he followed Roscommon's advice – 'seek a *Poet* who *your* way do's bend' – but this often meant he could avoid the use of poetic, that is, linguistic, intelligence. The *Selected Translations* begins with about ten pages of the libretto for a projected opera based on the *Tibetan Book of the Dead* or *Bardo Thödol*. They are 'included here because of [their] intrinsic merit and also because of [their] evident significance for Hughes himself'. It is not clear what their 'intrinsic merit' is, however. Weissbort describes them as 'relating to and involving translation' rather than as translations, but prints as an appendix four lines which appear – the book has not been well edited and there is ambiguity on this point – to be from Evans-Wentz's version of prayers to the Buddha. 'To the Divine Body of Truth, the

Incomprehensible, Boundless Light … obeisance.' This sounds more like liturgy than poetry (or rather, since liturgy can be poetry, like what might be good liturgy but is bad poetry – bad because indifferent to the language in which it is couched). Hughes tinkers but does not improve:

A: To the Divine body of the Truth obeisance

A & B: The boundless incomprehensible light.

It is an uncomfortable start to the volume. Fortunately, the next item is a bit of the *Odyssey* – Weissbort gets the book right but the line-numbers wrong – and is full of life, wonderfully direct and physical in its language, as when Athene, ending a storm, 'Reined back all blasts from their running and bound them in stillness'. Compare Richmond Lattimore: 'She fastened down the courses of all the rest of the stormwinds,/ and told them all to go to sleep now and to give over …' If you check this against the Loeb translation ('She checked the paths of the other winds and bade them all cease and be lulled to rest') you can see that Lattimore is closer to Homer in making three clauses of it, but that his 'fastened down the courses' is clumsy periphrasis and his 'give over' awkward colloquialism. Hughes's 'reined back' is direct and natural and its force as metaphor is enhanced by the alliterating word 'running'. 'And bound them in stillness' makes one clause of two and to good effect; the action is more decisive, more god-like, for being more succinct.

The extracts from *Bardo Thödol* and the passage from the *Odyssey* illustrate two very different sides to Hughes's practice as a translator. The first clearly links with his belief in 'a Universal language', a language in which I find it hard to believe, whilst the second shows a poetic intelligence at work which is slighted by any great emphasis on 'literalism'. Weissbort writes of two divergent aims in Hughes's translations – 'free adaptation and … literal transcription'. Neither quite gives the poet his due.

Hughes could be an *intelligent* translator when he wanted to, and that seems to have been when he felt himself challenged in some way by the text with which he was dealing. Authors whose diction is stripped down, and whose position is anti-intellectual, as in the case of Pilinszky or Amichai or Sorescu, fit neatly with his idea of what poetry should be. He translates them convincingly, but his own contribution is hard to make out. By contrast, the fifteenth-century Italian of Lorenzo de Medici, in sentiment and expression so different from anything we can find in Hughes's *Collected Poems*, really had to be wrestled with, as we learn from a letter Weissbort quotes. Hughes writes of spending 'hours simply untangling the versions to correspond with my guessing at the 15th Century Italian, or even at the plain Italian of the original'. What will strike the reader is that he made an effort to find some equivalent for Lorenzo's rhymes. Hughes did not often rhyme. Here he substitutes half-rhymes for full rhymes but does not consistently offer them in rhyme-schemes as Lorenzo does; even so, something of the formality and harmony of the Italian poet comes over. They are not only part of the means by which he says what he has to say; they are part of what is said. Hughes has attended to the right detail, following Roscommon's advice to 'Take pains the *genuine* Meaning to explore'.

But he does not very often do so. His version of Racine ignores rhyme altogether, perhaps, as Weissbort suggests, because Lowell used it in *his* translation of *Phèdre*. The result is fluent and direct, but not a bit like Racine, whose rhymes imply a sense of occasion to which his characters must rise. Hughes's Hippolytus defends himself against the charge of lusting after his stepmother without conveying the offended princeliness out of which he should speak

> I do not wish to boast but, my lord,
> Above all other virtues, the one virtue
> That I was born to, and have been bred up to,
> Is hatred of this crime you charge me with.
> My aversion to it is a legend.
> Throughout Greece I am famed for just this.

Racine is capable of simplicity and directness, as David Gervais has reminded us recently, but that was not what he was aiming at here, where the pride and innocence, naivety even, of the noble speaker are mingled. Hippolyte speaks not of 'the crime you charge me with' but of the crimes 'they dare impute to me'. It is not that he does not 'wish to boast' but rather that he 'absolutely' does not wish to 'represent himself at too great advantage' (*Je ne veux point me peindre avec trop d'avantage*). Hughes is direct but flat. Lowell may be extraordinarily free; his Hippolyte is at least a complex character:

> I dislike praise, but those who know me best
> grant me one virtue – it's that I detest
> the very crimes of which I am accused.
> How often you yourself have been amused
> and puzzled by my love of purity,
> pushed to the point of crudeness.

'I dislike praise' is Lowell's invention, and so is 'amused/ and puzzled', but they are in line with the character Racine imagined (the first more so than the second). Hughes, we are told, 'was intent on conveying Racine's masterpiece as myth'; the result is something very much less than its original. The very idea that there might be a 'mythical' element to what he is translating seems to switch off his poetic intelligence.

That is what happens with his *Tales from Ovid*. There is not enough about them that is Ovidian. Hughes thought that the *Metamorphoses* established 'a rough register of what it feels like to live in the psychological gulf that opens at the end of an era', but he was simplifying, willing a parallel between Ovid and his own view of the late twentieth century that is without substance. The extract Weissbort gives from his account of Salmacis and Hermaphrodite begins like this:

'I've won!' shrieked Salmacis. 'He's mine!'

She could not help herself.
'He's mine!' she laughed, and with a couple of bounds
Hit the pool stark naked
In a rocking crash and thump of water –
The slips of her raiment settling wherever
They happened to fall.

This is a terrible hamming-up of the original two lines: *'uicimus et meus est,'* exclamat *Nais, et omni/ ueste procul iacta mediis immittitur undis* ... Ovid's succinctness is sly where Hughes is obvious at length. His 'rocking crash and thump of water' is noisy where Ovid's *mediis immittitur undis* murmurs, because *his* nymph is quite cool about what she is doing, cool as the poet who describes her. No need for him to say that Salmacis was 'stark naked'; the absoluteness of the gesture with which she casts off all her clothes is implied in the enjambement *omni/ ueste*, where *omni* at the end of the line has you guessing 'all *what?*' It could have been 'discretion' after all. You might call this teasing, and it is a kind of play with the reader, but the restraint is also a form of respect utterly lacking in Hughes. It is as though he supposed the intentness on myth would exonerate him altogether from attention to the details that cumulatively make Ovid a great poet. One might say simply that Hughes has re-made Ovid for the twentieth century. This is an argument better applied to the *Adaptations* of Derek Mahon, who does envisage an audience capable of registering nuance, as it seems Hughes did not. The vulgarity of Hughes's version is not so much a recapturing of the 'Universal language', to which he was so much attached, as the symptom of a 'psychological gulf' which was his own, though he wished to impute it more generally to the end of his era.

As 'an integral part of Hughes's creative and professional life', then, his translations tend to expose the weakness of his anti-intellectual position. Its strength is also visible, notably in his version of Seneca's *Oedipus*, for Seneca was violent and extreme in ways that Hughes was able to re-create for a twentieth-century audience. He found in Seneca a poet who *did* bend his way. Indeed, Hughes's reputation as a translator might have been better served by a re-issue of *Oedipus* than by the random sampling of the whole career Weissbort opted to give us. Too often the reasons for choosing one passage over another are unclear. Why are the excerpts from *The Oresteia* all from the *Agamemnon*? Why, in Cassandra's appeal to Apollo, are the comments of the Chorus, a vital part of the scene, suppressed? It is the Chorus that gives meaning to such otherwise empty lines as 'Apollo! Earth! Oh/ No. No. No. Apollo!' Nevertheless, readers will be grateful for things like the previously unpublished passages from Hughes's *Gawain and the Green Knight* and, more generally, for being reminded of all that Hughes, a man of great generosity, did, not so much *in* translation, as *for* translation. It is to be regretted that his own practice was too often to slight the work he was dealing with in the name of 'myth' and 'literalism'. His devotion to those ideas, his primitivism, made it difficult for him to manage his great gifts to the benefit of those he translated. Furthermore, it must, together with the disasters of his personal life in the late sixties and seventies, explain the very restricted, if distinctive and important, nature of what he was able to achieve in his own work.

No such depressing conclusions emerge from a consideration of the role of translation in the *oeuvre* of Derek Mahon. *His* writings are pervaded throughout, and to an unusual degree, by poetic intelligence. Some might feel that there is intellect rather than intelligence in the often dense allusiveness of his later poetry, but they would be wrong. Mahon finds a home, not just a reference library, in the Western poetic tradition which he knows so well. He feels it as much as he thinks about it. His translations reflect a keen awareness of what verbal art is. The details that constitute poetic success do not pass him by, because he has judgement and, in ways that were not possible for Hughes, knows himself. He has dissected his mind and examined every nerve.

Still, his new book is called *Adaptations*, not *Translations*, and surely not just because another Irishman got to the second title before him. 'These pieces,' he says, 'aren't translations, properly speaking, but versions of their originals devised, as often as not, from "cribs" of one kind or another.' For the reader, there is a bit of unhelpful ambiguity here: is the point that he is offering 'versions' rather than 'translations', or is it that he has depended – but not all the time – on 'cribs'? For the poet, the ambiguity may be helpful because it allows him not to seem to claim too much, and yet to avoid focusing on any particular weakness. His ostentatious diffidence ('poets use it [adaptation] to keep the engine ticking over') is a way of averting any evil eye on the part of the reader. It is also a way of putting Lowell into our heads; his *Imitations* also were supposed to have kept the engine ticking over ('written from time to time when I was unable to write anything of my own'). A book on a level with Lowell's does not turn up every day. *Adaptations* is such a book.

Mahon is just as free with his originals, on occasion, as Lowell was. Two of the versions of Sappho in *Imitations* are described as 'really new poems based on hers'; Mahon's 'Brecht in Svendborg' is accurately described as 'a piece of *bricolage* if ever there was one'. This is not typical however. Mahon usually reproduces an original, but with no pretence of 'literalism', even in the versions of Jaccottet, printed opposite the French when first published. (Only three of them are reproduced here from the 1988 collection; the whole set is still available from Gallery Press as *Words in the Air.*) He makes no secret of being free with the work of his poets ('I've taken many liberties'), yet gets even closer to them than did Lowell. It all has to do with attention to detail, to judgement, to the emphases that supreme poetic art can achieve.

The comparison between Mahon and Lowell is not difficult to make, since both poets have versions of Rimbaud's 'Le bateau ivre'. However, Mahon's special quality as adapter and translator does not come through as strongly in the case of Rimbaud as it does elsewhere. Rimbaud's poem is overwhelming; Mahon works hard and successfully to give the impression that he is overwhelmed. That makes his version untypical in an important respect; it is designed to conceal his poetic *intelligence*. A rather less overtly challenging adaptation – of 'The Cloud' by Pushkin – is more representative in the way it shows Mahon managing his resources, thoughtfully, as an artist. Here is the first stanza:

The storm is over and done.
A last cloud hangs alone,
the final puff of smoke
in a blue sky, its dark
shadow the last to limp
from forest, field and swamp.

The effect is one of simplicity (there are no words of more than two syllables), but of a simplicity qualified by the artfulness of the half-rhymes and the way the second sentence hesitates, extending itself finely, thinly, to the end of the stanza. These might be words for a latter-day Schubert to set, eschewing the large gestures of the German Romantic poets he made use of. Yet their relation to Pushkin's Russian is not straightforward. Pushkin uses a four-line stanza with a much longer, twelve-syllable, line, and his rhymes are full, his rhythm emphatic. More to the point, he uses syntax quite differently, so there is no fading extensiveness about that second sentence. Indeed Pushkin makes a sentence of each of the last three lines, and his emphasis on the solitary nature of the cloud is highly rhetorical – these lines all begin with the Russian word for 'alone'. Pushkin is more like Schubert's originals. Maurice Bowra catches nearly all these aspects of the original in a strikingly faithful version:

Last cloud of a storm that is scattered and over,
Alone in the skies of bright azure you hover.
Alone with sad shadows you float on your way,
Alone you throw gloom on the joy of the day.

But this faithful version isn't half as good as Mahon's. The 'bright azure' and 'sad shadows' are clichés, and although the right word is at the beginning of the last three lines, its effect is diminished by the strong rhythm driving on to the resting-place at the *end* of the line. It is a bit of a shock to find that the Russian has no equivalent for either Mahon's graphic verb 'limp' or his 'forest, field and swamp', absences faithfully rendered, as it were, by Bowra, but it is hard to regret them. Could it be that in adapting Pushkin Mahon has *improved* on him? He has certainly *remade* him, and was, I think, quite right to do so. The strong rhythm and full rhymes of Pushkin's poem are part of a Russian concept of verse that can't be carried over simply into English, and Mahon in writing for the twenty-first-century reader does the right thing in jettisoning them. His short lines, half-rhymes and sensitive sentence-structure replace Pushkin's emphasis on aloneness with an equivalent, delicate yet fully deliberated force. The blue sky is there, the shadow is there, only Pushkin's 'triumphant day' is absent (and even Bowra fudges that).

No doubt, part of the meaning of Pushkin's poem is its historical status – that it was written where it was when it was – and that must be largely untranslatable. His cloud is a Romantic cloud, like Wordsworth's in 'Daffodils', like Shelley's, like Palmer's 'Bright Cloud'. It is a cloud pregnant with Romantic emotion; we have access to it as part of history, though it may not be that we come to it *because* it is part of history. Mahon's cloud, on the other hand, belongs to his and our contemporary circumstance. In *Adaptations* it looks backwards to 'Lucretius on Clouds' and forwards to Brecht's 'White Cloud'. Only in this way does it imply its historical nature. And behind all three of these poems stands another – the poem in *Harbour Lights* (in which the Lucretius and Brecht also appeared) addressed to Mahon's youngest child, intimations of whose being are at first hazy, cloud-like, rich with uncertain portent, and who enters life 'like one of Aristophanes' cloud chorus'. That association is not available in *Adaptations*, but is replaced by another which is close to it – creative metamorphosis. Clouds change shape, bear rain, bring fruit; their showers are 'a multitude of life-germs, water sperm'. Stranger still, clouds, like poems, come, or seem to come, out of nowhere, and return to that nowhere also, like Pushkin's: '... slowly you drift away/ on a leaf-relieving breeze./ There's not a cloud in the sky.' Mahon's cloud-translations are a homage to the creative principle itself. They come close to essential Romantic doctrine but present themselves in a post-Romantic guise, more modest and more sparing of melodic riches than they would have been at an earlier time, but subtle and enchanting for all that.

The poems in *Adaptations* are arranged in chronological order, starting with Sophocles and ending with Nuala Ní Dhomhnaill, so that there is an emphasis on historical progression. It presents a view of western literary tradition, but without undue insistence. In this tradition the major themes are those of Romantic poetry – love, creation and exile – but treated in a cool, almost classical spirit. Mahon offers one adaptation from the Italian of Michelangelo; a sonnet about 'the image hidden in the calcium carbonate'; one of the meanings of its inclusion seems to be that Mahon himself is a sculptor, cutting into the bedrock of western culture. He aligns himself with the classical tradition which was Michelangelo's and, like Michelangelo, transforms it. He is very much in the line of Pound and Davie, one who carves rather than one who moulds. His interest in the poetry of the troubadours confirms this link and brings out the musical purity, the definition of consonant and vowel which is one of his finest qualities:

> When in spring the days grow long
> I listen to birds' distant song;
> Out on the road again I go
> Crippled with vain desire ...

But the best example of his sculptural attack is one with which many readers will already be familiar, his versions of Cavafy. These are based on the fine translations by Edmund Keeley and Philip Sherrard, which one might have thought could not be bettered (despite their assimilating the early poems, which used rhyme, to the free verse that later became the poet's norm). In their version of 'Voices' Keeley and Sherrard strike the note of unhesitant clarity and of irony that refuses shame which, thanks to them, English readers are accustomed to thinking of as Cavafy's:

Loved, idealized voices
of those who have died, or of those
lost for us like the dead.

Sometimes they speak to us in dreams;
sometimes deep in thought the mind hears them.

And, with their sound, for a moment return
sounds from our life's first poetry –
like distant music fading away at night.

Cavafy's Greek, also unrhymed, has much longer lines than this. Mahon, however, abbreviates the Keeley/Sherrard version, brings the rhythms much closer to the spoken language, stressing the final syllable in every case but one, and changes the last two lines round, so that, instead of counterpointing 'return' and 'fading away', they bring to the fore an idea of life which is very close to Mahon's own in his early poems (and this version is a relatively early work):

Definitive voices of the loved dead
or the loved lost, as good as dead,
speak to us in our dreams
or at odd moments.

Listening, we hear again,
like music at night,
the original poetry of our lives.

The result may fairly be compared to Michelangelo's cutting through the block to the image within. Of course, this is not Cavafy entire – but then, not even Keeley and Sherrard can give us that. What it may be is Cavafy in essence, the original poetry of his life to which his poems seek to give us access.

Adaptations is a very special book because it reflects a very particular and personal relationship to the western literary tradition. (In his foreword Mahon regrets the absence of poems from 'Spanish, Hebrew, Arabic, Ibo, Hindi or Chinese'; it is difficult to feel that this regret is profound except as it concerns Spanish). The poems from Pushkin, the troubadours, Michelangelo and Cavafy surely all have special significance for this poet, who elsewhere shows himself immersed in European culture, not merely its poetry but also its music and painting. So it is too with the versions from the French. His translation of Nerval's 'Chimères', first published in 1982, is here in its entirety, and there are three versions of Baudelaire, one of Laforgue and Rimbaud each, two of Valéry , two of Beckett's 'Burbles' and three of Jaccottet. The (commissioned) translations from Molière, Racine and Rostand are not represented (though some of the *tirades* from *Phèdre* certainly deserve more notice), and neither is the slightly awkward version of St-John Perse's *Birds*. Perse is very difficult to bring over into English. Nevertheless Mahon's attempt is worth getting hold of (again, from the valiant Gallery Press) because it says so much about Mahon's own poetic aspirations, which have to do with Symbolist apprehensions of another, or perhaps an original, life:

> Even now a God hides among bricks and bones –
> and, like an eye closed in the womb, a pure
> spirit evolves beneath the glaze of stones!

This is from Nerval's 'Pythagorean Lines', of which Mahon had already made use before he published his translation. The perilous fashion in which 'pure/ spirit' bridges the line is his touch, rather than Nerval's, and says a good deal about him, both in the vulnerable exposure associated with purity, and in the sense of dissipation that accompanies the arrival of 'spirit'. There is nothing remarkable in claiming purity for what you can neither see nor handle, though there may be something doubtful about it, which is why, though 'pure' loses force as it predicates 'spirit', the sense of anxiety persists.

Mahon's most direct assault on French symbolism is his version of 'Le cimetière marin'. It is 'a masterpiece' according to the dustjacket of *Harbour Lights*, and, up to a point, I agree. Valéry's poem is eloquent, grand and obscure, and so is Mahon's. Yet there is a nervous quality about the English version that is missing from the French, or so it seems to me (this is true also of the Nerval). Take the opening of the poem. The French is:

> *Ce toit tranquille, où marchent des colombes,*
> *Entre les pins palpite, entre les tombes …*

which is translated with tolerable accuracy (by Graham Dunstan Martin) as 'This peaceful roof where doves are walking/ Pulses between the tombs, between the pines'. The 'roof' is the sea, and the doves are boats sailing upon it, so Mahon offers

> A tranquil surface where a spinnaker moves
> flickers among the pines, among the graves …

This has a great deal to be said in its favour, in particular the choice of the visually alert 'flickers' for *palpite* and the disorientating effect of putting the two verbs 'moves' and 'flickers' together. It is a restless opening, the spinnaker forward in the mouth, flying free of the depths and anticipating the sound of the first word in the second line. It is quite unlike, *essentially* unlike, Valéry, whose first line is almost entirely at the back of the mouth, connoting depth and, perhaps, mystery. It is only after some time that Valéry's reader understands that roof and doves are metaphoric, and the moment of understanding should be like an emergence from the depths into the dazzling light of the sun. The whole poem is about the movement of a consciousness, and for this reason the initial move from metaphor to that which the metaphor shadows or expresses is of great importance. The *sound* of the poem also matters as a quality of the mind that is conscious within it. Valéry said of this very poem (again I use the translation of Graham Dunstan Martin):

Poetic necessity is inseparable from palpable form, and the thoughts stated or suggested by a poem's text are not at all the sole and vital object of speech – they are *means* which combine *equally* with the sounds, cadences, rhythm and ornaments to produce and sustain a certain tension or exaltation, to engender in us a *world* – or a *mode of existence* – that is entirely harmonic.

Thus Mahon's version is very much what he terms it, an *adaptation*, one that expresses not Valéry's consciousness but his own, one that longs for the assurance and power of the French original, but that manages something very slightly other. In doing so, Mahon conforms to Valéry's own views as to what a poem is ('Once published, a text is, so to speak, a mechanism which everyone can use in his own way and as best he can'; 'I have written a "score" – but I can hear it only when it is performed by the mind and spirit of another'). Nor can it be denied that what Mahon produces is a *grand* poem, one with the confidence informing Valéry's own. The deep harmonies of the French original are replaced, as we have seen, with something more brilliant and forward, as though the sea signified more than the darkness beneath the trees. It is allowable in the way that productions of Shakespeare set in the Napoleonic wars or the Arctic wastes are allowable if they light up something in the text we might have missed, as we might say that Mahon's half-rhyme of 'moves' and 'graves' picks up on the meaningful syllabic imbalance of Valéry's *colombes* and *tombes*, which the very harmonious quality of the French can conceal from us. It is as though the key has changed but essential relations are maintained.

It is still possible, though, to question how *much* that is essential has got through in Mahon's version. His title, *Adaptations*, suggests that he might think that some of his remodelling amounts to fundamental restructuring, and some readers might agree with him. The last stanza of Valéry's poem begins with the famous line *Le vent se lève! … Il faut tenter de vivre!* Graham Dunstan Martin offers 'The wind rises! … Life calls to be attempted!', to which you might prefer C. Day Lewis's version: 'The wind is rising! …We must try to live!' But neither is really satisfactory, because the French impersonal verb *il faut*, which harmonises so well with the metaphysical concerns of the whole poem, cannot be reproduced in English. 'Life calls' is a good attempt, but it isn't *il faut*. Then again, Valéry's line ends emphatically on a long vowel, forward in the mouth, where the English equivalent, 'live', has a short vowel, which can also be emphatic but cuts out the aspirational feeling of *vivre* by making a different demand on breathing. It is quite clear that Mahon is aware of this difficulty, and he juggles with the following line in order to end the first one with a long vowel, indeed the same long vowel as Valéry's. But he is only able to do this by introducing a briskness to the statement of necessity that simply isn't there in the French:

the wind rises; it's time to start. A vast breeze
opens and shuts the notebook on my knee.

This is extremely beautiful, but has a grittiness that belongs to the Irish poet more than the French one. Some readers will feel that 'it's time to start' just travesties the yearning quality of what Valéry actually wrote. Others will recognize that translation is invariably interpretation and judge that Mahon's alert and inventive handling of the original – the phrase 'a vast breeze' is particularly striking and meaningful – in the end brings us close to one of the meanings the poet would most have been pleased for us to find in his poem – 'Such Secrets are not easily found out,/ But, once Discover'd, leave no Room for Doubt.'

The choice of poems for Mahon's *Adapatations* is not merely haphazard. Their arrangement in chronological order of original composition suggests that the reader should be on the lookout for development and variation amongst them, that there is an Idea of poetry in the western tradition, or a set of ideas about that poetry, lying behind the book. Many of the poems have a meaning also in relation to Mahon's own work. He includes a great deal from within the French symbolist tradition – Nerval, Baudelaire, Rimbaud, Laforgue and Valéry account for more than a quarter of the book's length, a way of saying that Symbolism has a privileged place in Mahon's view of poetry. His own poems often reflect a need or desire for some alternative order to that which the world he inhabits immediately presents. Nerval's 'pure/ spirit' evolving `beneath the glaze of stones' could naturally appeal to a Belfast-bred child, the poet of `Glengormley'. If that makes the poet sound too much at the mercy of his surroundings, too much a victim of the cult of the drifter and outsider, then the fact that the book begins with choruses from Sophocles should set the reader on another track. The chorus from *Antigone* has already been translated by Heaney in *The Burial at Thebes*; that from *Oedipus at Colonus* is the one that Yeats included in *The Tower*. Mahon is claiming his rightful place among Irish poets. The *Antigone* version is particularly interesting because it is more dramatic than Heaney's, even though it has here to stand alone. Heaney's Chorus is eloquent in praise of man, 'Home-maker, thought-taker, measure of all things', reserving for the end the warning that he must abide by the law of the city – if not, 'He'll have put himself beyond the pale./ When he comes begging we will turn our backs.' But in Mahon the Chorus do not speak from a position of advantage; as they seem to in *The Burial at Thebes*. They praise themselves under the guise of 'man': 'Our wide-ranging resources,/ so beneficial' and so on. The tired phrases have a point which becomes clear in the stanza Mahon adds to this chorus:

With speech and intuitions
born in the lightning brain
we create civilizations,
shelter from wind and rain.
Each difficult circumstance,
crisis, disease or pain,
inspires us; only against
death do we strive in vain.

The juxtaposition of 'civilizations,/ shelter from wind and rain' mutely pleads on behalf of the vulnerable beings who trust in what they call 'Our visionary technology'.

It is all 'shelter from wind and rain' – not just the technology on which civilizations base themselves, but the 'visionary' arts, like the art of poetry itself, which are supposed to be the crown of those civilizations. Opening with this poem, Mahon's *Adaptations* places itself in the midst of the human dilemma, not above it, and with a seriousness that certainly equals, if it does not outweigh, that of Heaney.

Mahon triumphantly vindicates Roscommon's view that 'They who too faithfully on *Names* insist/ Rather Create than *Dissipate* the *Mist*.' Pretty well wherever you consult the originals from which he has worked (I have to make an exception for one of the Baudelaire versions) you find a great poetic intelligence at work, one that does not feel it beneath itself to ponder and judge the detail of his authors. This never comes through as an obtrusive intellectualism, however. I do not think that Hughes would have withheld his praise. There is little of the 'intrusive, formal, merely communicative … element of language' here.

Examining just how Mahon has read his chosen authors, I was often reminded of Donald Davie's beautiful poem 'The God of Details', depicting an autumn garden:

No need to gloss the reason
Why thus punctiliously
In madder and in lemon
Leafage precipitates.

Mahon's book is not autumnal. If I have too punctiliously glossed the reasons for its specific colouring, that is because arguments about 'literalism', like many of the themes of 'translation studies' tend to obscure the quality of genuinely creative translators. But what I have glossed has all the beauty and variousness of the leaves rained down in Davie's garden:

… its dried-peel, amber
Distractedly, profusely,
Yet sparsely, and yet sparsely.

But is it Davie's garden? The poem is, after all, 'after Pasternak' – one of the poems of the 'Afterword' to his *My Sister Life*. Is it a close translation? I think so. Then is it Pasternak? Can it be Pasternak if it does not rhyme, does not incorporate his prolific word-play, does not reproduce his stanza-form? It is Davie-Pasternak, just as Mahon's 'White Night' and 'Earth' are Mahon-Pasternak. There is something essential for both Davie and Mahon in this relationship, which has to do with the compatibility of their work and the Russian's. Henry Gifford wrote of Pasternak that 'the task he sets before poetry is to recognise particulars, and to harmonise them through the imagination'. That is what we find in Davie's 'God of Details' and in Mahon's *Adaptations*:

I do not know the riddle
Of the pitch dark past the tomb
But Life is, as the autumn's
Hush is, a minuteness.

William Bedford

Observation Transformed Into Vision

Neil Roberts, **Ted Hughes**: *A Literary Life* (Palgrave Macmillan, 2006)

Neil Roberts's argument in *Ted Hughes: A Literary Life* is simple. Accepting that the tragedies of Sylvia Plath and Assia Wevill 'will always, in the public mind, be the "main plot"'(p.2), he sets out to show that there 'is another "plot", more deeply buried, more far-reaching and possibly more central to Hughes's vocation as a poet, that would have made his literary life far from straightforward even if his personal life had been less tragic' (ibid). This deeper story has to do with notions of a 'lost paradise, and associated idea of the Fall' which 'became a template for Hughes's *Weltanschauung*, and especially for his construction of the history of Western civilisation' (ibid). Hughes 'was profoundly at odds with the secular, rational and materialistic culture in which he lived' (ibid), and in exploring his spiritual dilemma, Roberts makes an interesting case for Hughes as a poet working firmly in the tradition of Eliot and Yeats.

Much has been made of Hughes's time at Cambridge, especially the dream-visitation of a fox, a central image in Hughes's mythology. But over Hughes's lifetime there were in fact three such visitations, and Roberts is excellent in unravelling the key texts. The publication history of these pieces is misleading, but biographically, the incidents they describe occurred as follows. In the short story 'The Deadfall' (1), the young Hughes is called to rescue an injured fox, and is rewarded with a bone carving of a fox. In the short prose piece 'The Burnt Fox' (2) a second call is described in the dream-visitation of a fox while Hughes was at Cambridge, and again the poet responds, changing course from the study of literature to anthropology. Most intriguingly, at the very end of his career in 'Epiphany' (3), we are told of yet a third visitation, this time around the time of the birth of Frieda Hughes, when the adult poet failed to meet the challenge symbolised in the gift of a cub fox. Whether retrospectively or not, Hughes felt that he had received a call to the shamanic life, and during his marriage to Plath had failed to respond to that call.

None of this would have been apparent to the early readers of *The Hawk in the Rain*. As Roberts says, 'it is unlikely that at this time (Hughes) knew much about shamanism' (p.20). The volume is interesting for rather paradoxical reasons. Despite the chorus of praise that greeted its publication, in fact only a handful of poems represent what came to be seen as Hughes's authentic vision. These are the best poems in the collection – 'The Horses', 'The Hawk in the Rain', 'Wind', 'Jaguar', 'Meeting' and 'October Dawn' – showing 'the human protagonist . . . threatened or diminished by natural energy' (p.23) and exploring 'the usurpation or invasion of the world that the rational intellect has constructed, by a power that is represented as greater and ultimately more real' (p.28).

Even more interestingly, as we shall see when we look at Plath's intervention in the writing of *Wodwo*, the most famous and successful poem in the volume, 'The Thought-Fox', is perhaps the least characteristic of Hughes's best work. Roberts is in no doubt that 'Apart from a strained pun on the paw-prints of the fox and the printed page, which unfortunately determines the last line' the poem is 'entirely successful' (p.21). Quoting the following lines:

> warily a lame
> Shadow lags by stump and in hollow
> Of a body that is bold to come
> Across clearings . . .

he argues that the 'poem does not *say* that the fox's shadow is distorted by the irregular terrain over which it passes. Rather that sense-impression is completely saturated by the figurative displacement of the fox's natural fear on to its shadow, leaving the fox itself free to represent a bold venturesomeness. The separation is reinforced by the literal separation of the shadow from the body and by the rhythm: the dragging, front-heavy stresses of the first complete line quoted, in contrast to the rapid anapaestic rhythm of the second, and the leap across the stanza-break' (pp.22-3). These are the conventional techniques of English prosody. What is interesting about their deployment, and seems to have infuriated Plath, was precisely the uncharacteristic formal restraint, and the 'image of the poet, or his persona, embodying a "wise passiveness"' (p.23) within the poem.

Between June 1957 and December 1959 Hughes and Sylvia Plath lived wholly in America, where most of *Lupercal* was written. What is intriguing and significant here is that none of the poems of this volume reflect the American landscapes in which they were written. Indeed, they are written as if the poet is still in England. Unlike D.H. Lawrence, Hughes did not seem to respond to his time in America, regarding it as 'a barrenly spiritless time' (p.54). With Hughes, 'one has the impression of a writer intently preserving an inner resource' (p44). The use of memory, implicitly of childhood, is also important . . . it is central to three of the finest poems in *Lupercal*: 'View of a Pig' and 'The Bull Moses' (p.45), and perhaps most importantly to 'Pike', where the 'depth signified by the pond is at once autochthonous, imaginative and temporal', becoming 'still more resonant in the final stanza when the pike that the young fisherman is fishing for in terror becomes' (p.46):

> The dream
> Darkness beneath night's darkness had freed
> That rose slowly towards me, watching.

The '"Darkness beneath night's darkness" echoes the "deeper within darkness" of 'The Thought-Fox', but the 'unsatisfactorily neat conclusion of 'The Thought-Fox', "The page is printed", betrays an evasion of the actual gulf between a fox and a fairly traditional, though excellent poem. The conclusion of 'Pike', quoted above, is much more open. The poem ends on a present participle, an uncompleted action, and the speaker is threatened rather than fulfilled by the imagined predatory creature' (ibid).

'Yet the pike, no less than the fox, is a manifestation of creative power' (ibid), Roberts goes on to say, and in these words we see the beginning of the theme that obsessed Hughes throughout his career. Hughes's argument about the hawk and the pike is that they are 'at rest in the law' (p.49), their killing being part of the natural order, and he has written compellingly about this law 'and the ways in which it is violated by our "customary social and humanitarian values"', (ibid). In *Lupercal*, Roberts suggests, 'this power is precisely the inner resources that the poet is desperate to preserve' (p.47).

By the time *Wodwo* was published in 1967, Hughes's 'inner resources' must have been under considerable stress. There is some confusion as to the dating of the poems, but they were clearly written during the marriage breakdown and after Plath's suicide. With the privilege of hindsight, we can also see that the issue of shamanism becomes central in these years, although readers at the time could be forgiven for missing the clues to what was a largely hidden and very complicated story.

To deal with shamanism and its significance for *Wodwo* first, Roberts has some interesting things to say about the author's note to the volume 'telling the reader that the book is to be read "as a single adventure"'. It is a note which 'has caused problems for readers ever since it was published', the adventure being difficult if not impossible to identify 'because it is intensely private and imposed on the book retrospectively' (p.57). Hughes himself has said that 'the central event (of the book and of his life from 1961-62 onwards) is the "invitation or importuning of a subjective world" which he refuses, the consequence of which refusal is "mental collapse into the condition of an animal"' (p.57). As Roberts points out, Daniel Hoffman was one of the few people at the time to recognise 'the "adventure" as the call to the shamanic life', and it is important to bear in mind Mircea Eliade's judgement that "'once chosen by the spirits . . . there is no other life for you, you must shamanize or die"' (p.58). We have already seen how the fox functions within Hughes's own mythology as the messenger bringing this call to the shamanic life, and though the interpretation is, as Roberts shows, retrospective, it is perfectly clear once pointed out. 'The poems in the first part belong to the period before the event, when he had an "undisturbed relationship with the outside natural world", the stories are "episodes of the event", and the poems in the final part are after the event' (pp.57-8). The "'single adventure" is of more obvious interpretative value in relation to the stories and the play than to the poems' (p.59) but a careful reading of Roberts's argument seems to me to prove the point. Whereas the hero of *Sir Gawain and the Green Knight* – from which Hughes finds his title - accepts the challenge he is faced with, Hughes clearly felt he had somehow failed to respond, and in the final poem 'Wodwo' 'the protagonist of the "single adventure" suffers "a mental collapse into the condition of an animal"' (p.61).

As far as the poems themselves are concerned, one of the most interesting and significant passages in *Ted Hughes: A Literary Life* comes when Roberts is discussing 'the influence or inter-textuality of Plath and Hughes' (p.64) with specific reference to the poem 'Wodwo'. As Roberts says, 'In the poems written after Plath's death we can see for the first time the aesthetic of ugliness, a challenge to poetic norms, that is to become much more conscious and systematic a few years later in *Crow*' (p.67). Returning to 'The Thought-Fox', he points out that Plath's poem 'Burning the Letters' was written on the verso of a typescript of Hughes's poem: in the words of Lynda K. Bundtzen, Plath's poem is '"an anti-thought fox"' poem (p.65) written in the free verse of *Ariel*. Plath is quoted as rejecting the formal style, the '"poetic lyricism"' (ibid) and '"literary convention"'(ibid) of the Hughes poem in favour of '"the poetic efficacy of shrieks – Something crude and sensational"' (ibid). With her 'raw evocation of the fox's death' (ibid), Roberts himself continues, in the 'extremely loose form of free verse' (p.66) she had been evolving, Plath can certainly be interpreted as attacking both Hughes's vision and 'neatly constructed' (p.66) form, and even if '"ugliness" is not an end in itself' (p.67), 'the same freedom that made the *Crow* poems possible also enabled Hughes to write 'two of his most radiant celebrations of the natural world' (ibid), 'Skylarks' and 'Gnat-Psalm'.

There is certainly a new-found technical freedom in these poems. As Daniel Hoffman is quoted as saying, in *Wodwo* Hughes '"abandons stanzaic and metrical conventions for line-breaks and the spacing of bursts of lines which try to capture the shape of experience"' (p67). This is outstandingly exemplified in these lines from 'Skylarks" (ibid):

A towered bird, shot through the crested head,
With the command, not die
But climb
Climb
Sing
Obedient as to death a dead thing.

Roberts goes on to argue that here 'the formal freedom is combined with great sensitivity to rhythm and intonation. The lineation of the short lines creates pauses which map them rhythmically on to the longer line that follows. At the same time the rising pitch of "Climb . . . Sing" enacts both the literal rise and the transformation of effort into musical utterance, while the rhyme "Sing / thing" creates an unsettling double effect, echoing the utterance while reducing the lark to an object' (p.68).

There are many poems of this quality in *Wodwo*, and whether we are persuaded by the evaluations being offered here or not, it seems obvious that the explication of both the religious and technical changes in Hughes's work is irrefutable. That same explication presents the critic dealing with *Crow* with enormous difficulties. The very incompleteness of the volume as we have it is part of its achievement, but if we want a complete picture of the process of writing, and the consequences of that very incompleteness for the rest of Hughes's career, we do need to grasp the wider context. Given this complexity, it might be best to start with Roberts's basic judgement of *Crow* as we have it:

> In this chapter I shall be arguing that the particular impact of *Crow* as a volume, its effect of shock, provocation, occasionally outrage, its arousal of an unanticipated kind of aesthetic pleasure, its combination of desolation and sometimes raucous humour, and of exquisite poetic skill with deliberate crudity, is dependent on its incompleteness, fragmentariness and undecidability. It invokes the worlds of myth and folktale, but has none of the explanatory power of myth (p.73).

The problem for explication is that we have the published *Crow* 'and a number of other texts and rumours that surround it and potentially destabilise a reading of it' (p.72). 'The function of the "story"', Roberts argues, 'is to close down interpretation of the poems, to control their enigmatic, provocative quality by hitching them to a moral' (p.76), whereas generally 'the poems work best when kept free of the narrative frame' (p.77). Part of this narrative is to be found on the recording Hughes made of *Crow*, and Keith Sagar put together a more complete version from various notes and public readings, to be found in his *The Laughter of Foxes*. From these various sources, it is clear that 'at least some of the time that Hughes was writing *Crow* he conceived it as an epic folk-tale, and that his plans for the narrative were very ambitious' (p.79). Keith Sagar believed that '*Crow* would undoubtedly have been one of Hughes's greatest works had that project not been aborted in 1969' (p.72) after the deaths of Assia Wevill and their daughter Shura. But I think Roberts is right, when he says that the problem with the narrative framework is that it is itself 'fragmentary, often desultory' and bears 'only the most vestigial relationship to the ambitious narrative scheme' (p.73).

So what is the aesthetic achievement of *Crow*? A large part of the effect has to do with the 'super-ugly language' (p.73), the 'relentless mesmeric chant' of Biblical parody, the 'savage momentum' and 'hint of tragic nihilism and absurdly grotesque juxtaposition' (p.74), which alienates unsympathic critics. But as Roberts suggests, a line such as 'Trembling featherless elbows in the nest's filth' is also 'a beautifully concise evocation of an actual nestling', one of the 'most outstanding examples of the style of *Crow*, with its rhythmically assured shift from the falling, dactyllic opening to the abrupt, spondaic conclusion, and the gathering together of the consonants of the trisyllabic "featherless" into the monosyllable "filth"' (ibid). There are many such lines in *Crow*, but the poems are too well known to need much quotation, and I can only agree with Roberts when he claims that 'few poets could equal' the beauty of a line such as 'When the curlew trawled at seadusk through a chime of wineglasses' (ibid).

It seems to me that Roberts makes a clear case for *Crow* as one of the necessary masterpieces of the twentieth-century, but there is little doubt that Hughes's sense of failure and being 'cursed' (p.1) inhibited his work in the coming decade. In the 1970s, Hughes was exceptionally prolific, the years 1973-1976 seeing the publication of *Gaudete, Cave Birds, Season Songs, Moortown Diary, Adam and the Sacred Nine, Orts* and 'Caprichos' (p.102). The obvious explanation for this perceived failure was the 'public outcry about Sylvia Plath' (p.85), and one of the many fine things about *Ted Hughes: A Literary Life* is Roberts's handling of the feminist maelstrom into which Hughes's private life took him. His chapter on 'The Plath "Wars"' makes salutary reading.

There is no need to rehearse the arguments here, but the most significant 'literary' effect can be seen in *Gaudete* and *Cave Birds*, both of which 'centre on female victims and a guilty male protagonist' (p.99). Roberts makes an interesting connection between Hughes's personal tragedies and his wider philosophical view of some 'crime' or 'error' (p.101) which he 'associates historically with Socratic rationalism, monotheism, the Reformation and the scientific revolution' (ibid), the issues explored discursively in *Shakespeare and the Goddess of Complete Being*

I am not entirely convinced by Roberts's argument regarding *Cave Birds*, which I have always found damagingly obscure even with the Baskin illustrations which are so crucial to the meaning. These illustrations are not included in *Three Books* or the *Collected Poems*, which doesn't help matters, but part of the problem may well be that the work is 'unusually densely allusive' (p.114) without the more immediate aesthetic rewards one finds in *Gaudete*.

But as he was exploring his own shamanistic mythology, Hughes was also writing the apparently much simpler poems of *Season Songs, Moortown Diary* and *River*, where we see the poet as practical farmer and fisherman. These poems show the human as being 'no longer eclipsed by the animal' and the animal as no longer predatory: 'The human has a greater awareness, and may occasionally be able to help, but mostly can only look on in baffled sympathy' (p.124). Some of the most significant of these poems are in the volume *River*. Here, in a brilliant analysis of 'That Morning', Roberts concentrates on the 'religious' vision many critics have found in this collection, explicating lines such as 'Solemn to stand there in the pollen light/Waist-deep in wild salmon swaying massed/As from the hand of God' (p.144) with a skill that is a joy to read.

> The emotive and religious gestures of this passage are anchored in the artistry of the second line quoted. The pattern of assonance and alliteration combines with a spondaic rhythm that is the opposite of 'bludgeoning'. The predominance of semivowel, sibilant and nasal in the spondaic stresses produces a soft, surging, rather than abrupt, movement, while the interweaving of assonance and alliteration binds the words into a whole suggestive of massive, mobile fluidity (ibid).

'That Morning' has always seemed to me one of Hughes's greatest poems, the moment when 'Two gold bears came down and swam like men' (p.145) indeed one of those 'moments' when literature changes our way of seeing.

Hughes was a creative artist for almost fifty years, but it was not until his final years that he produced the collection which seemed to resolve many of the dilemmas which had distorted his career. Roberts discusses *Birthday Letters* 'as poems of explanation, self-justification and mourning' (p.201). The poems of explanation and self-justification are clearly the most destabilised by the Bakhtinian dialogic nature of literary discourse – especially given the public nature of Hughes's experience – and Roberts analyses their relative failure extremely well. But it in his discussions of the poems of mourning that he makes clear the greatness of some of the *Birthday Letters* poems, particularly and for me most movingly, 'Visit', one of the finest poems in the collection.

The analysis here is not so much to do with prosody as with narrative structures. What Roberts is trying to explicate in his discussion is the way Lacan's '"strange temporality" . . . explicitly superimposes the past on the present of writing, in which the mourning subject is directly glimpsed' (p.209). 'Visit' explores 'a moment ten years after Plath's death in which Hughes, reading her journal, experiences "The shock of your joy" on learning that he was in Cambridge. The journal entry is described as "Your actual words, as they floated / Out through your throat and tongue and onto your page" – a powerful phonocentric transformation of the written record . . . into the lost one's physical presence. This effect is reinforced by a logically inconsequential but emotionally compelling link . . . with another moment when the child Frieda . . . suddenly asked, "Daddy, where's Mummy?" The link is an emotionally complex one. Hughes was "there" both literally and supportively for his child, which he was not for Plath either at the moment of her journal entry or at her death, and the daughter's voice is a literal memory, whereas Plath's is an illusion . . . created by the processes of mourning. The poem shifts back confusingly to the night in 1956 when Hughes tried but failed to visit Plath, but sensed "Our future trying to happen"', before returning 'to the present of the mourning subject', and the final moving words (pp.209-10):

> I look up – as if to meet your voice
> With all its urgent future
> That has burst in on me. Then look back
> At the book of the printed words.
> You are ten years dead. It is only a story.
> Your story. My story.

There may be problems with Hughes's passivity in these elegies, there may be problems with the determinism with which he understands Plath's fate – an understanding he expressed in different ways throughout his life – but it would take a profoundly ideological and vindictive reading to see these elegies as anything other than deeply moving. Roberts's reference to Shakespeare and Hardy is relevant, but the poem that came to my mind was Henry King's extraordinary 'Exequy'. It may take some time before we can read *Birthday Letters* without being 'destabilised' by its historical and biographical context, but it contains several of his finest poems.

There is something refreshing about the tact, insight and common sense with which Neil Roberts approaches Hughes's life and work. The controversies surrounding the private life are in no way evaded, but such 'facts' as are known are discussed with a sensitivity which puts to shame much of the biographical speculation which has characterised responses to Hughes's career. Taking as much account of 'context' as might reasonably be expected by a fair-minded reader, Roberts frees himself to consider a body of work which challenges almost every aspect of our 'secular, rationalistic and materialistic' (p.2) culture. *Ted Hughes: A Literary Life* gives us true scholarship at the service of its subject, and it would be difficult to find praise high enough for Robert's marvellous achievement.

---

(1) Ted Hughes, 'The Deadfall', *Difficulties of a Bridegroom* (Faber, 1995), pp.1-19.

(2) Hughes, 'The Burnt Fox', *Winter Pollen* (Faber, 1994) pp.8-9.

(3) Hughes, 'Epiphany', *Birthday Letters* (Faber, 1998), pp.113-15.

Annie Charlesworth

Letter to the dead

(to Ted Hughes and Sylvia Plath)

To speak of the dead is to make them live
                    once again.
                              Egyptian saying

                         i

From the Old and New Kingdom of high-running skies
and woods crackling into a gold
                    unmeasured by time,

                    I send you tongues of Druids,
the sap of pines and hoofprints of flying horses
                    to place after your last line
                              in the infinite echoing spaces.

There – seeds of poems float
                              in baskets braided from papyri
on banks of streams,
stealing too late the current's green rhythms.

                    Yet cursives in your handwriting
keep in touch with her,
                    the treasure of voyeurs,
in ancient, almost indecipherable scripts

on cracked, terracotta bowls
                              and on linen patterned already
                    by tracks of claws.

                    Across, under, through and above
your lines,
with a meticulous reverence, you resuscitate her.

Atom by atom, ash by ash on cremation ghats
        and syllable by syllable
                you change her back
into a vowel, a consonant;

give her muscles the energy of verbs,
        roll her in stories, anecdotes, rhymes
and colours of children's building bricks:

blue, yellow, staining her new dresses
            with the red of her full lips.
You fill a wardrobe with outfits
        of old desires and destinies
hung from the ribs of goblins and ogres.

Hear the characters in her Tarot pack laugh
           when bears, bats and snakes
        cavort in a ring
centre stage instead of her.
           And you and she

at each other's mercy are the main predators –
        with shots, traps, bites and snares –
and victims of your words that ricochet
        off each other

like soul mates. How tenderly you take her hand –
its severed life-line
        awaiting sutures
you have never stitched,
        hanging

on the cliff edges of your grammar
           like a horizon upended.
How faithfully your images,
        some of which you steal from her,
blue in their faces,

           jolt her back into being
a sentence, a stanza, a page on a breath,
the lexis of a whole dictionary.

iii

Too many tortures: her fear, her panic,
her perfectionism,
                    the doll, her daddy the interceptor
  in your double bed
                        the electric shocks, the ghosts
demons

you her she you
                all descend into the labyrinth
of unlit thornbushes,
                    step by step down

to Minos in the middle who holds court –
the court of the underworld – counsellor extraordinary,
                    wielder of peace.
  Watch
with him the Minotaur, untied from its nose-ring,
                        head and horns lowered,
coughing up your flesh and hers
                    for you to paste onto new scrolls
made from the giant reed of many waters
                        which unroll and unroll.

iv

In the Old and New Kingdom of Pharaoh and Ptolemy
you inhabit anywhere,
                    everywhere
and she – your Isis,
                clever of tongue,

Lady of many names
                names you while you thump her chest
for a duple rhythm
                    then collect from folk memory
her DNA.

Who would recognise the kind of necrophilia
                you practise
or see the smoke from her diary
                        offering no amnesia
                while it burns into an alphabet
  its twisting tattoos?

Her turn to emerge from her shrine
of papier maché
and to parse you:
your irregular tenses and gerunds,

your scribbles on shards
of the belljar that she pieces together
before taking your hand
to guide into the shape of a joint signature.

There is linen still to be ironed into sheets –
for the silence of inhaling pines –
by the first light
of every day you shared.

There are feathers to be shaken
from pillows
for the migration of epistles and screeds,
and the banishment of poison pens
that punctuate your legend

in the infinite echoing spaces.
Let me send, for your deathdays, birthdays
full of chain letters you can swap
endlessly like daisies

heart to heart.
No tombs needed
for the Ogam and Egyptian print
in which flying horses propel your art.

William Bedford

Cold Stars

i.m. Elaine Connell 1953-2007

It's 3 a.m.

I'm thinking about you.

The sky is very full of stars.

The Aranda say the stars are holes in the sky to let the light in. Crows made the holes, pecking at the dark tin to escape this world. Other tribes say it was the magpies.

I miss you.

A white mist rolls across the hills and I'm also thinking about Sylvia Plath because she wrote about sheep in fog and you wrote a book about her grief, following her with your own grief.

All night, this morning has been coming.

It has been heading our way, you in Yorkshire, me in Wiltshire, the Aranda watching the stars, telling stories to quieten their fears.

Are we the only people awake?
The only people who watch for the morning?

It's 3 a.m., and I know you are listening, but I am alone with Sylvia Plath, and she is not listening, she is sitting round the fires with the Aranda, inventing new stories about the stars.

Making holes in the sky to let the light in.

W.S. Milne

A Standing-Stone

Michael Longley's *Collected Poems* (Cape Poetry, 2006. 346pp. £25.)

Michael Longley's poetry celebrates imagination and moral equilibrium. Of the first quality he says, 'I extend the sea, its idioms', and its 'Ten thousand hooves thunder in our ears'. One hears the voice of Cuchulain in that last phrase, the Yeatsian influence evident also in the poet's belief in language's power to transcend 'old boots and kettles for inheritance'. Like Yeats then, and like Joyce, Longley likes to re-work classical myths and tales into the fabric of modern life, thereby achieving a traditional balance, an equilibrium, which one also hears in the best poems of Heaney, Mahon and Montague, his equally fine Irish poetic contemporaries. The sonority of his poetic line rings out clearly with theirs. Like them, he is not inclined to give in to the powers of the world, nor is he tempted to forego craft in favour of popular pressure; rather, he is bent on establishing a classical idiom of balance and poise as a model of resistance to the pressures of the time. It is 'in this lively synthesis' of 'Body and Mind…Who house philosophy and force' that he forges a countermanding rhythm comparable to an ethical power which is pitched against the brutality and murder of much of contemporary reality. The poetic act in this context is 'a risk taken' in the face of the world, a hazarding of instinct and intelligence. This moral approach to the act of writing (it is more than a mere aesthetic stance for Longley) reminds me of the tensions one finds in the poetry of Allen Tate, John Crowe Ransom, and John Berryman, for instance. Longley writes of 'the frantic stars', 'delirium', 'fatal appetite', 'the lumber of my soul', 'my panic, my breathlessness', of 'balancing buckets of terror'. Against this Pascalian dizziness, these horrors, he opposes massive learning and poise. His translation and reading in this collection ranges from Homer, Virgil, Tibullus, Horace, through Old Irish literature, the English Metaphysical poets, Sir Philip Sidney, the Scots Gavin Douglas, Robert Fergusson, up to MacDiarmid, George Mackay Brown and Iain Crichton Smith, the Englishmen Auden, T. S. Eliot, and Ted Hughes, and such modern European authors as Leopardi, Baudelaire, Montale, Celan, Cavafy, Sorescu, Pavese, and Pascoli. The range of reference is impressive.

Repose, harmony, pose: these are Longley's gods then, and they are hard to find in a world torn apart by sectarian murder and strife. In writing of The Troubles (and no-one has written better about them than Longley) he has gone back to the great war-poems of Charles Sorley, Keith Douglas and Edward Thomas, amongst others (including Homer, of course), for his models. And this is his strength. He doesn't think that he can lash out at the powers-that-be ('everything that soul-destroys' as he puts it) on his own: he knows he has many noble compatriots in the struggle, and he calls upon them to help. In this way 'the storm' of imagination is 'contained' by the 'rigging 'and 'netting' of tradition. The poet's field of vision remains focused, precise:

Unmarked were the bodies of the soldier-poets
For shrapnel opened up again the fontanel
Like a hailstone melting towards deep water
At the bottom of a well, or a mosquito
Balancing its tiny shadow above the lip.

It was rushes of air that took the breath away
As though curtains were drawn suddenly aside
And darkness streamed into the dormitory
Where everybody talked about the war ending
And always it would be the last week of the war.

('The War Poets')

War is 'the mincing machine' the peaceful poet however must resist from
praising – 'the wolf treading its circuits towards sleep'. Pose, elegance: these are
the qualities Longley admires, and those he embodies in his poems. We have to go
back I think to Yeats for this measure, his 'Night can outbalance day', 'I balanced
all, brought all to mind', 'beauty like a tightened bow', 'sinew that has been pulled
tight', 'measured quietude'. It is this very counterpoise then Longley attains in his
own poetry, and it seems to me a tone largely, unfortunately, missing from most
contemporary poets' work. They seem often to mistake anger and rant, at times,
for intelligence and craft, and, of course, there is a world of difference between
them. The movement of his poetics is 'from flux to poise, from poise/To attitude',
a phrase that surely has its roots both in Heraclitus's philosophy and in the verse
of Gerard Manley Hopkins. Equilibrium then in the face of chaos, this is what is
required of the morally courageous poet, 'As winds are balanced in a swaying tree/
I cradle your cries'. Peace requires home and shelter, a place to feel safe, and so it
is Longley praises the hearth and domesticity, the charms and consolations of his
native Irish countryside, the townland, its 'lares', its 'sheltered branch':

Dawns and dusks here should consist of
Me scooping a hollow for her hip-bone,
The stony headland a bullaun, a cup
To balance her body in like water:

Then a slow awakening to the swans
That fly home in twos, married for life,
Larks nestling beside the cattle's feet
And snipe the weight of the human soul.

(from 'In Mayo')

He takes time out in a considerable number of poems, for instance, to praise the ancient art of quilt-making, and the tradition of embroidery that stretches all the way back to *The Odyssey*. Likewise Longley, like D. H. Lawrence, is especially interested in the peacefulness of the creatures, especially of birds, and celebrates their natures on nearly every page:

> When you weighed against
> A dried-out wine cork
> The goldcrest, then buried
> The twelfth of an ounce
> Which was its eye, feathers
> And inner workings,
> Did you release, love,
> Among the tree tops
> The ghost of a bouquet?

('Goldcrest')

In this sense his rural verse is often akin to the best of Austin Clarke, for example, or of F. R. Higgins, or of Patrick Kavanagh. Paramount, however, for Longley is the hymning of human love (or of its losses), the central theme of his poetics – love pitted against the huge forces of fate and necessity, 'steered along the night':

> You define with your perfume
> Infinitely shifting zones
> And print in falls of talcum
> The shadow of your foot.
>
> Gossamers spin from your teeth,
> So many light constructions
> Describing as with wet wings
> The gully under my tongue.
>
> These wide migrations begin
> In our seamier districts –
> A slumdweller's pigeons
> Released from creaking baskets.

('Love Poem')

Longley's art praises what he calls 'the fundamental interconnectedness of all things', and his vision is embodied in the lines of a master-craftsman. He champions the love lyric and the pastoral over war's threnodies ('all the dreary epics of the muscle-bound', he calls them), but without diminishing the realities of the latter, either in his own nation's 'blood-saturated ground' or in that of other nations' 'odour of blood on the ancestral stair'. He seeks, and often finds, communion in remote Irish localities, and celebrates 'the confluence of lines' there, the intermeshing of cultures, the meshing of lives – a 'village of minds', 'poetry's townland', 'a whole community':

Because you've built shelves across the big window, keep-
Sakes and ornaments become part of the snowy garden.

The footprints we and the animals leave in the snow
Borrow the blue from the blue glassware you collect.

I imagine your dead husband moving in and out
Through window and shelves without breaking a thing.

He is the snow poet and he keeps his snow shoes on.

('Maureen Murphy's Window')

There is an American influence that can be traced in Longley's work (one can hear the voices of Roethke, Frost, and Stevens, for example, in some poems, but incorporated, made Longley's own) and again, I would argue, this shows the poet's cosmopolitanism, a necessary balance to his rural themes. He is a poet of courage too, standing out against anything that smacks of the ephemeral, or of the trivial. Poetry, for him, is the art of 'Twisting straw into a golden cable,' and that action can be seen at work in his best poems (some of them very famous, rightly, and much anthologised) such as 'The Linen Workers', 'The Butchers', 'The Echo-Gate', 'Northern Lights', 'Hallowe'en', 'Aftermath', 'Washing', 'An Amish Rug', 'The Eel-Trap', and 'A Bed of Leaves'. Like Yeats's poems, Longley's are 'rooted in one dear, perpetual place', Ireland, 'wherever life pours ordinary plenty':

If you were to read my poems, all of them, I mean,
My life's work, at the one sitting, in the one place,
Let it be here by this half-hearted waterfall
That allows each pebbly basin its separate say.
Damp stones and syllables, then, as it grows dark
And you go home past overgrown vineyards and
Chestnut trees, suppliers once of crossbeams, moon-
Shaped nuts, flour, and crackly stuffing for mattresses,
Leave them here, on the page, in your mind's eye, lit
Like the fireflies at the waterfall, a wall of stars.

('The Waterfall')

Michael Longley's poetry 'reconstructs/Broken voices, broken stones, history' in an incomparable fashion, and for him 'Where science ends and love begins' that's where poetry starts.

Patricia McCarthy

A Question of Androgyny

'androgyny of angels, edges to a circle'...
from 'Of Shadow: Of Simile' by Eavan Boland

Eavan Boland: *Domestic Violence*, Carcanet 2007, £8.95
Eavan Boland: *A Sourcebook*, Edited by Jody Allen Randolph, Carcanet 2007, £12.95
Fiona Sampson: *Common Prayer*, Carcanet 2007, £9.95

To address the question of reputation or fame: if having a *Sourcebook* full of poems, prose, interviews, reviews and criticism, published by Carcanet Press in tandem with your latest collection which has followed your *Collected Poems* means that you are on examination syllabuses and are entitled to be called by Americans 'Ireland's foremost woman poet', then so be it. Eavan Boland is, without doubt, at her best a strong, distinguished poet but she has done little justice to herself in several ways. Firstly, her insistence on being 'Irish' and a 'woman poet' (a male poet is not, after all, called 'a man poet') who gives a voice to all the ordinary silent women in Ireland's past and present has meant that she has been trapped in what her contemporary, poet and critic Carol Rumens calls 'the Anglo-American feminist tradition', which sees Boland as doubly oppressed as 'Irish' and a 'woman', quite possibly 'to the detriment of her talent'. Secondly, the fact that she seems wrapped in the 'Irishry' concocted by and applauded by many American academics who seize on Irish poets, especially marginalized 'woman poets', precisely because they can fit them into the politically correct and politically popular category of survivors of 'The Troubles', causes her to be viewed with suspicion and questioned for her authenticity on this side of the Atlantic. She can hardly lay claim, as Americans seem to think she can, to being an oppressed, exiled 'Irish woman poet' who has suffered atrocities while living in a comfortable middleclass suburb of the capital city of the Republic which, even at the height of 'The Troubles', physically escaped the trauma and bloodshed almost entirely. Thirdly, the radicalism that Boland claims for herself – to make appropriate as a theme for poetry the ordinary lived life of the Irish woman – surely belongs to the feminist novels and poetry of the 60s and 70s, but is outdated today. A contradiction lies in Boland's claim made as early as 1993: 'I couldn't be a feminist poet. Simply because the poem is a place of experience and not a place of convictions.' Yet in 1995, in an interview with Jan Garden Castro, she stated: 'I'm a feminist but not a feminist poet' and, almost in the same breath: 'I now think a woman poet can be a mainstream political poet'. What kind of blarney is this?

Selected and edited by Jody Allen Randolph (an American), this *Sourcebook* is both enlightening and disappointing. Extracts from Boland's prose are not always well-chosen, since too much is over-repetitive and full of contradictions.

Yet Boland's prose – behind her lofty pose as a spokeswoman for her nation – both in the interviews and in the prose pieces is articulate, interesting and full of rhythmical cadences. She says somewhere that her prose and poetry represent a single continuum and illuminate each other. Countering the nineteenth century view that no one 'should ever intrude on the interpretation of a poem', she takes pride in saying 'Often as a slight subversion of it, I'd title the prose piece the same as a poem. I want to suggest the continuity of these processes.' Her radicalism again? This has been done often before via notebooks, letters, journals. What about Rilke and Virginia Woolf, to name but two authors? There are some gems here for those who write poetry, for example: 'Some of the real indexes of where poetry is, or where a particular poet is – is how far the voice is pushed against the line.' And there are samples of fine poems of hers from her main collections, showing the influence of Yeats early on, then Sylvia Plath and Anne Sexton ('Anorexic', 'Domestic Interior', 'Night Feed', 'Mise Eire'). However, the somewhat affected grandiloquent and bald proclamations, which ring hollow, riddle her work intermittently throughout and detract from it. For example, in 'Anna Liffey', she declares portentously, 'It has taken me/All my strength to do this.//Becoming a figure in a poem.//Usurping a name and a theme'. Or what about this? 'In the end/It will not matter/That I was a woman. I am sure of it'. Or even worse in her latest collection, *Domestic Violence*: 'We failed our moment or our moment failed us./The times were grand in size and we were small'.

In a trenchant review of *Domestic Violence* in *Poetry Ireland*, issue 90, Maria Johnston comments 'Boland's tenth collection of poetry, *Domestic Violence*, does little to convince of her talents as a poet'. And, after accusations of 'a self conscious heavy handedness', 'a jaded flatness', 'a bland sameness', 'pomp and hackneyed philosophising', Johnston comes out with: 'the poems speak of experiences but never become experiences in themselves' – damnation for a poet (Boland) who was convinced in an interview in 1995 that, 'as a mode of experiencing an experience, poetry is excellent'.

Domestic Violence certainly gets one's back up with its misleading title which is in poor taste since it parodies real domestic violence and could be construed as a cheap sell, encouraging not only voyeurs but also those victims of domestic violence who, often inarticulate, might be helped by a poetry dealing with such harrowing issues. Boland's justification is a throwaway token sentence, showing no understanding at all: 'I wanted, imaginatively and figuratively – and only, of course, in the realm of the poem – domestic violence. I had a deep respect for the customary use of the term to denote a tragic relationship'... Surely it is this 'customary use of the term' that she slights with her complacent 'ordinary' life and bourgeois privileges, and in wanting the domestic poem, in her hands, to 'advance' by her reinterpretation of it. 'To speak aggressively of its reality from its private world'. New territory? What about Sylvia Plath, even if her 'private world' was a distorted one?

In this sequence, Boland is at her best with a sharp, microscopic focus, and in her elegies, but at her worst when pseudo-grand, over-explanatory, and forcing a big Irish theme. There are brilliant, moving, finely achieved poems such as 'How the Dance came to the City', 'How It Was Once In Our Country', 'An Elegy for My Mother In Which She Scarcely Speaks', 'Amber', 'And Soul', 'Letters to the Dead', 'Indoors' and 'In Coming Days'. Though she seems too hooked on the past, mostly on Ireland's past, her historical research is thorough, including the lexis attached to the specific era. For example, the formally-written poem, 'Violence Against Women', set, for once, in England, in the Pennines, concerning the drudgery of mill girls who would have been represented in fantasy in English pastoral verse of the time, is both well researched and very well achieved. It has a greater number of levels than many of the poems here, and draws finely to an end with the invocation of 'art' and 'empire' (grand addressees, it is true): 'tell me what it is you have done with/the satin bonnets and the pastel sun, with/the women gathering their unreal sheep/into real verse for whom no one will weep?' In 'Letters To the Dead' the successful focus for the poem is 'the old Kingdom' she has researched whose scholars found words written on pottery and called them 'letters to the dead'. In other poems, she cites the particular dates which lend an authenticity. Yet when she is more factual than suggestive, the impact of her work which is, after all, well crafted, is lessened. When she lets her images assume their power to be impressionistic and not spelt out, she can be extremely effective, such as the last part of 'Falling Asleep to the Sound of Rain'. She wants to live, she says, where the first emigrants lived: 'Their country was a finger to the lips, a child's question stopped./And yet behind their eyes in eerie silence, was an island,/if you looked for it: bronze-green perch in a mute river.' It is a pity, given the strength of this, that her work is too often declamatory and forced, too often prosaic and attempting to make a 'big' poem about Ireland (it would be interesting to count the number of times the word 'Ireland' or 'Irish' turns up in this sequence), using the first person plural as 'the spokeswoman', let us not forget, 'for the age'. Too often she is an over-conscious narrator forcing a 'story'. Seamus Heaney talks about 'the angle of saying' and I am not sure that her 'angle' is always the apppropriate one. She needs to let her images speak more from behind themselves – as she can do so well – so that different levels and layers of meaning emerge from them instead of her platitudinous, over self-conscious proclamations which keep the text at surface level only and force the reader into a single reading – the poet's own – of the poem. In the poem, 'Still Life', about an emigrant just after the Famine who went from Clonakilty to Philadelphia and became a painter, she concedes: 'I believe the surfaces of things/ can barely hold in what is under them'. She is referring to an etching – of an Irish beggar woman with a dead baby in her arms. Nevertheless, these lines show, even if only in her subconscious mind, that Boland is aware of the importance of suggestive levels which, as 'woman poet' Carol Ann Duffy proves, do not necessarily need to be put into words, but can be articulated through different tones. Maybe Maria Johnston is right: Boland needs to move into a greater freedom and a music that speaks through different tones and forms as well as through its melodies, away from all posturing whether historical, mythic, national or feminist, 'past the tired boundaries of gender, of ideology that have for so long marked out her territory. The mind is not gendered, nor does the voice of the poem have to be, but Boland's strategies never allow the reader to forget that it is this "woman poet" that speaks.' Listen to how effective she can be when she does step out of her role, for example, in analysing memory in the resonant poem 'Amber':

as though the past could be present and memory itself
a Baltic honey –

a chafing at the edges of the seen, a showing off of just how much
can be kept safe

inside a flawed translucence.

In her early, Yeatsian, more formalist poems such as 'Athene's Song', 'The War Horse', and 'Child of our Time' she seems to have been ashamed of the androgynous approach encouraged in women's writing early in the century by Virginia Woolf in her essay 'A Room of One's Own' where the latter posits that there won't be a female Shakespeare until women write androgynously, as she herself did in her prose-poems of novels. In an interview in 1993 Boland shows her denigration of the 'genderless poem' actively proposed to her by male poets who 'would say things like "the best thing about your work is that you would never know it was by a woman"'.

In her new collection, *Common Prayer* (Carcanet, £9.95), Fiona Sampson moves some considerable way past Boland's 'tired boundaries of gender and ideology' and demonstrates the magnetic power of a 'genderless' mind that navigates the numinous and the material realms through articulate, startlingly original images. She composes an androgynous music that modulates sonorously from abstract to concrete and from concrete to abstract and back with crescendos and diminuendos, and demonstrates the phrasing and intonation of an intellectual poet/violinist familiar with musical scores. Unlike the broken lines of Boland's free verse which are delivered in general in a monotone, and often fix the 'ordinary' and the 'domestic' images on a simplistic, superficial level, Sampson's broken lines and atonal rhythms at times are reminiscent of Stravinsky or Prokofiev. Specific poems, also, are linked directly to composers, such as 'Attitudes of Prayer' which is '*after Beethoven, Quartet in C# minor, Op 131*', other poems have titles such as 'Messiaen's Piano', 'Night Fugue' and 'Nocturne in Blue and Black'. The latter contains 'bell-like notes of John Cage' and an exhortation: 'Think of chimes falling on an anvil of air/that clangs back, upward – /each bell-stroke returned//to the echo-roof;/the wide Vale suspended//between breaths, between strike/and release.' The strong poem 'Scenes from the Miracle Cabinet' concerns the hospital 'world of illness', where clinical language is effectively juxtaposed with refrains from the Old Testament, including the Song of Solomon: '*Saw ye whom my soul loveth?*' set to the rhythm of the hospital lifts going up and down through different levels with '*Doors opening*' and '*Doors closing*' in 'pain's nerve-lament/Dark, voiceless music'. And, in the parallel hospital poem, 'The Plunge', concerning a vigil in hospital, showing sensitive understanding of how illness makes outsiders of the sick, the clipped 'Draw the curtain./ Beds fill, empty and fill' is concluded by the rhetorical question of outrage and injustice: 'Is there any music to justify this?' The 'black river' – that a heron seems to swallow down like an eel – leads to 'I feel the river's long/cold on my skin' and 'You've placed fear on my finger, /caged river-bird'. These lyrical but eerie images are threaded through the reality of body parts, 'the loneliness of your naked body' and 'you become unknown even to yourself', to exert a kind of mock contrapuntal music in this stark poem. The conclusion: 'Your fear/ and mine/ make a verse with no answer' shows that even the music of poetry is impotent in such a situation.

Recurrent images, too, such as the light, mirrors, glass, a widening and contracting lens, silk, the colour white, along with biblical and liturgical language provide leitmotifs which unify the sequence with the kind of orchestration T.S. Eliot used in *Four Quartets*. Indeed, Eliot might well have been proud of Sampson as his protégée in taking up the legacy he left to poets after him: of how to inject music into poetry. Sampson's way of doing this, however, is very much her own.

The whole book represents a kind of interrogation of light by the musician, the artist, the scientist, the philosopher, the weaver, all of whom comprise the single poet who, through a variety of lenses, allows the subtle 'light' of her language to transcend the mundane and banal, even to give it a numinosity. As John Kinsella so succinctly says: 'She can elevate the ordinary, and settle the elevated', an approach Boland might do well to adopt. It is difficult to quote from bits of poems because they move all of a piece and build up as they flow, so that the whole poem needs, ultimately, to be quoted. For example, from the poem 'Mehr Licht', a routine act such as hair-washing becomes an extraordinary, analytical, universal, epiphanic experience. There is too much light 'tremoring/ beyond vision' which causes both fear and awe. This light exerts a strange power 'in the kitchen laboratory' where it gains a weirdness by being personified: 'will light just lay itself down in cellular instance,/green, brown;// will it strip itself out/in the shine of a plate?' Querulous wonderment is found 'under the lenses/of soap-bubbles –/ Is this radiance?' But terror sets in again and the light seems possible of causing radiation, of causing burns, hair to 'shrivel to a flowing pointillism', eyes to 'turn to glass', the tongue, 'a glitter of carbon' will 'frost your mouth', reminiscent of Hiroshima. 'What you're afraid of –/pulling rays down into yourself/on the kitchen doorstep –/so that, secretly ignited, /radiation/will transfigure you. At the sink/when you run hot water/over glass already webbed with wet,/light refracts –// a shadow/passing over the lens/with the whirr of migrating birds:/ *further, further,/* they whisper'. At the same time 'into the concrete L/between house and kitchen/sunlight flocks in a kind of Möbius wave/ and return,/a continual pulse-less flow and exchange'. By the end of the poem the whole head of hair and even the light are transfigured: '...*look /* waves of colour-particles/are washing your hair, they're thrown streaming/ down your back –/

soundlessly/the whole scarf/of light; the pulsing crown.'

In *Domestic Violence*, Boland touches on analysing language in the honed poem 'Instructions', which mainly concerns the ageing process of – you have guessed it – a woman: 'Now take syntax. Break that too. What is left is for you/ and you only'. In 'The Origins of Our Native Speech' what was a 'nation of fever' becomes a nation perpetually fearing 'contagion' that only fire can cleanse, 'the words we spoke/coming back to us/fractured by delirium'. She is very hard on 'The Nineteenth-Century Irish Poets' and, in a poem of that name, sees them in retrospect: '…I think they were poisoned –/ every word they used contaminated by the one it was not'. She now reads 'every line as if it came from a burned throat' and concludes: 'Now I see what it is they left us. The Toxic lyric.//The poem for which there is no antidote'. More delicately, perhaps, she wonders why no one 'crouched to hear' the language of the singing kettle: 'its rising shriek in winter or wrote it down with/the birds in their blue sleeves of air/torn away with the trees that sheltered them'. Why didn't she do this? She talks about having 'nothing to assist me but the last/and most fabulous of beasts – language, language' – and then movingly adds: 'which knows, as I do, that it's too late/to record the loss of these things [i.e. all the things associated with her mother after her death] but does so anyway,/ and anxiously, in case it shares their fate'.

Sampson is less specific than Boland and more forward-looking in her approach. For her, language explodes everywhere. For example in 'The Looking Glass', she asks:

> Or does this in fact have to do with language?
> The way it hooks, draws in,
>
> every name
>   a displacement?
>
> The nib in your hand's a crochet-hook
> pulling things across,
>   making starry combinations;
>
> and if you've lost the knack, other generations
> will move your fingers –
>
> The sea has a special language:
>
> Easy to exchange an elephant-hide Atlantic
> for this mercurial Med,
>   this dazzler
>
> whose urgent narratives from the middle of the world
> slur against your bare feet

Even a stone, with 'its vein of glitter' is 'parsable under your finger'. She gives a grammar, too, to abstracts. In 'Fogbound', for example, the light has a voice: 'light sibilates along them;/ here, here it whispers,//smudgy with echo'. Elsewhere she mentions 'breath's/ dangerous vocative' and 'the future perfect of loss'. In another poem the springs of 'a borrowed bed' 'are texting, through my bones.' In 'La Source' there is 'a wide-screen sky'. In one of the erotic and tender love poems 'Take, Eat', formally written, she dares to link the communion of two lovers with liturgical communion, in a kind of metaphysical conceit, which is extended with the play on 'case': '...Capitalised Name//or nipple raised to Upper Case –/that taps your palate, jinks a toast/in soft communion – the boast/your mouth's the same in either case'.

Sampson surely shows here, in Boland's words, 'how far her voice is pushed against the line'. With her accurately directed 'angle', not only of 'saying' but also of 'seeing' and 'hearing', she takes much greater risks than Boland and shows Boland up for being too confined by her 'Irish woman' and 'the past of the Nation' myth that the latter has helped construct around herself.

In her wonderful handling of textures, through adjectives, word coinage, repetition, sometimes alliterative and assonantal, Sampson reminds one of Gerard Manley Hopkins. For example she speaks shockingly accurately of 'puckered water', 'the whicker-flight/of geese'. Like Hopkins, she also seems, perhaps subconsciously, to define 'inscape'. In 'In Carinthia', she describes 'how each thing pulls inward to self –/catkin, white violet –/and toward each other' – which harks back to Hopkins' sonnet, 'As Kingfishers catch fire': 'Each mortal thing...Selves –/ goes itself; *myself* it speaks and spells'. The up and down movements of images and feelings in this sequence also recall Hopkins' gymnastic verse. Boland rarely shows such swings, though when she does, she is very successful. In the fine poem, 'Indoors', for example, she says articulately, 'There is always a place where a fable starts – where a god/proves he is a god by adding/not simply wings and sinews to his shoulders//but the horizon swinging up – rivers, mountains, headlights/ only slowly/ righting themselves as he rises to find/ the first signs of day becoming night'. Why does she not do this kind of thing more often?

In Sampson's sequence there are snatches of quotations from other poets, skilfully interjected. The bits learnt by heart which have become part of the poet can be slotted into her own verse as if her own. In the excellent, strangely erotic poem 'At the Sex Frontier', addressed to a ghost soul-mate who eludes touch because there is a pane of glass between them, there is a whisper, along with all the other whispers in these pages, of Baudelaire: 'mon semblable, mon frère'. Rilke is not far away either in the line 'things unalterably themselves' from the telling poem 'The Earth-Wire' full of redolent images such as '...and now woods return/as if everything can be mended,/as if pine needles/can knit it back together' and 'Scratched with snow-leavings, a slope/ unbends millennia'. In 'Trumpeldor Beach' the angels responsible for triggering epiphanies could be Rilke's own:

These are the fictional angels,
these bursts of supra-natural radiance
you could put your hand through;
that melt
    at the shadow of your foot
when you try to step in
to accept their cold
brilliant baptism.

Pablo Neruda, the great poet of the love lyric, could be the persona in number 2 of 'Blood Lyric', though this lyric is surprisingly sparse and honed: 'Did you kill me/or love me?' and it is laudable that Sampson is unafraid of passion.

A snatch from T.S. Eliot's *Four Quartets* is inserted aptly into the fine poem 'Attitudes of Prayer': 'Early December./Grey on grey, grey annealing grey,//except light catching the high/ notes of a fiddle/ *(quick quick said the bird)*:/Your breath/ like smoke on the window'. This bird must be the bird from *Four Quartets* who introduces the garden in the opening passage of 'Burnt Norton'. Among other places, there is a distinct passage about the Tube in 'The Looking Glass': 'that woman knitting on the Tube,/her hands flicker and pass, flicker and pass', and you 'had to let her go/with the swollen faces in the ads sliding behind her'. The emptiness, and weirdness of the Underground is slightly reminiscent again of passages in *Four Quartets*: 'And here it is again:/a mute, spatial awareness//of how things are,/unlearnt, unearned'. The 'strange seeping-away clatter/of the Underground' invites a mantra: 'Edgware Road, Regent's Park,/Marylebone –//wayside shrines/on your journey in the dark'. This recalls a similar list of underground stations in *Four Quartets*, illuminating the wrong way of travelling in the wrong sort of dark.

In the accomplished poem 'Common Prayer', which bears the title of this sequence, as well as the extraordinarily original image-making, there are telling lines. Here, Sampson is not (but could well be) speaking about her own voice: 'That voice/testing the palate of the void/was yours'. She could also be (but isn't) redressing Boland for compelling herself to belong to an Ireland in order to hold herself secure in the corset of poetry that she feels she has a duty to handle: 'It's not about belonging. You don't *belong*./ It's about the landscape/as confessor'. Again, in 'Fog-bound', where 'fog binds the world/ with cold-as-charity bandages' and exudes an 'oozy bloom', the universally applicable short passage:

    Fog shields you –
it's a kind of caretaking
that reduces big questions
      to presence

involves the 'fog' most human beings reside in, not being awake enough to penetrate man's materialistic complacency which prevents a higher state of awareness being reached, according to the Eastern Masters such as Guridjeff and Ouspensky. Alternatively – and this demonstrates the elasticity of meaning inherent in any poem, and the possibility of many different readings – the 'presence' could mean the actual abstract attainment of this higher awareness. The first interpretation of course could well apply to Boland's deliberate 'Irish woman' pose which does prevent her from expanding into the fullness of her talent. Ironically, it is Boland's own words about fog, from her poem 'Falling Asleep to the Sound of Rain', that demonstrate that she is capable of extending into multi-layers and levels other than that 'way of seeing' connected with Ireland and its history: 'We love fog because/it shifts old anomalies into the elements/surrounding them. It gives relief from a way of seeing.// It is the gift of sleep or the approach to sleep,/to make component parts of place and consciousness/meaningless and, as breathing slows down//to do what water does, announce a source in cadence,/repetition, sound, allow a gradual dissolving of/ boundaries between the actual and evident and still'.

Despite their differences, then, both poets share themes such as death, displacement whether through illness or history, even images such as 'silk', the colour 'blue', and light. Boland's poems are more drenched by rain than, like Sampson's, suffused with light, but Boland does show an original eye for light. Her 'traveller' is a 'long/polished scrap of light' from 'an age of ice and nothingness'; the two figures on a long-owned blue and white mug have 'their own weather' and most likely 'do not know when light is rearranged/according to the usual celestial ordinance –/tides, stars, a less and later dusk'.

Both Sampson and Boland assess the body's role in our strange mortality. In the very moving poem 'And Soul' which shows Boland at her best, and concerns her mother's death in one of the wettest summers on record, the poet cleverly reduces the body to the water that 'the body is' which surrounds her – rainwater, sea-water, river water, the vocabulary for the different kinds of water 'inside our speech'. The poem hauntingly reduces itself, it seems, as the mother's body is being reduced by death: 'fog into mist,/mist into sea spray and both into the oily glaze that lay on the railings of/the house she was dying in/as I went inside.' Elsewhere, she speaks of her own, and any woman's ageing, and contrasts this with the 'truths of the body' suddenly discovered sensuously and secretly by a young girl in the exhilarating poem, 'How the Dance Came to the City'. The question she asks in 'Formation' could be Sampson's own:

What is the body anyway but a stranger
bringing news of somewhere else?

Sampson focuses more on the abstract body of light and its different slants on and illuminations of the human body, including its parts. In 'The Looking Glass' this is pleasurable, for example, and in the contrasting hospital, it is traumatic. The experience of being a visitor on a ward makes her realise we are all naked under our clothes, even the healthy, going up in the hospital lift 'into our incurable selves'. She shows how the body can be changed by experience and sometimes there is a choice. The visitor to the acute ward walks out either 'in a new skin,/shining all over' or ends 'on a scaffold bed/among scraps of hallucination'. She movingly defines the body that is desirable despite the ravages of illness: smoke 'smells of you –// of your smoker's body,/ which I want to touch/ with all the artifices of compassion; /in which I want to touch/ our common name'. Set against this, in the daringly erotic poem, 'Body Mass', is the glorified body of desire wrapped in religious language. 'Each bone's a chalice: each gleaning thigh/ a high-lipped cup', even though 'desire's nothing personal'.

Both poets also focus on 'the local'. In an essay in *The Sourcebook*, Albert Gelpi attributes Boland's 'success' partly to her validation of the American conviction articulated by William Carlos Williams that the local is the universal, and this, together with the 'Irishness of her work', says Gelpi, accounts for the reciprocated affinity she has found with American poets. How strange, then, that Boland, in *PN Review*, albeit in 1990, denigrated 'the local' in stating that the details of Ireland's past, the hunger and angers, 'however terrible, remain local', promoting merely 'the hollow victories, the passive images, the rhyming queens'. She valued, she said, in these details, the human truths of humiliation and survival, the complex suffering of Ireland's 'defeated' women at 'the deepest, most ethical level'. The problem here is that in *Domestic Violence* many details used by Boland herself seem only surface. For example, as a woman of a Dublin suburb, she refers repeatedly to Dundrum where she resides, to a Dublin that she romanticises yet writes very lyrically about in her prose, and which in her poetry includes the Dublin hills, Dublin Bay, a Dublin evening, the river Liffey above Leixlip, Howth. Clonakilty in West Cork also features, and New York, Long Island and Philadelphia are touched upon in passing. Her most interesting use of 'the local' occurs, however, in her predilection for 'small towns' and for the fantasy small town in the fine poem 'The Room In Which My First Child Slept', similar but different to Yeats' imaginary 'Lake Isle of Innisfree'. This poem has an interesting pattern in which the magically conjured small town, known for its calico, appears with memorable details such as snow, a river, 'coarse daisies' and a 'red-billed bird' trying to land. The little town then disappears because it never existed, yet, inexplicably, the poet keeps hearing the river 'making /its way through the dusk, having learned to speak the way I once spoke, saying/ *as if I didn't love you/ as if I wouldn't have died for you.*' The closing rhythmical mantra confirms this poem as one of enchantment and tenderness. Boland should work this territory more often into her poetry. Another poem, 'Falling Asleep to the Sound of Rain', a passage of which resembles Fiona Sampson's work in its eloquent treatment of water as an abstract which announces 'a source in cadence,/ repetition, sound', allows 'a gradual dissolving of/ boundaries between the actual and evident and still'. Her honesty is compelling. Despite all the claims to the place-names, she admits, 'I know there never was/ a single place for me. I never lost enough to have one.'

Sampson's poems move more globally through Europe's violent twentieth century, offering meditations on a whole world in crisis. She is aware of locality in terms of language that is struggled with: 'the revelation of scale/ as it moves through the local'. In her poem about desire, 'Body Mass', she defines desire and its fulfilment as anonymous: his cries 'belie/ how it's a local godhead that he meets'. The fact that the 'godhead' is 'local' seems to imply either that the singular 'we' in the final line of the poem means that 'a local godhead' has been reached by the lovers' union, or that sex as such, although it aims in a loving relationship to 'chase flights of angels', is earthy and limited, and rarely matches up to its expectations.

In the work of both Eavan Boland and Fiona Sampson, in the words of the American poet, Adrienne Rich, who, to Boland was 'an empowering forbear', what we see is 'the great muscle of metaphor drawing strength from resemblance in difference. The great muscle of the unconstricted throat'.*

---

*from Adrienne Rich's essay 'Poetry and Commitment': W.W. Norton & Company, 2007.

Chosen young Broadsheet essayist

Kate Edwards, 32, completed her PhD thesis, entitled 'Beyond Englishness: Culture and Context in Relation to David Jones's *In Parenthesis*', in 2005 at the University of Kent. She now teaches part time at the Centre for Continuing Education at the University of Sussex and is currently writing a book on the Jewish population of central Italy during the Renaissance.

The Revolving Epoch: David Jones and Oswald Spengler

The past is constantly present in David Jones's work. It is recovered in an archaeological manner, returned in fragments, no longer holistically inhabitable perhaps, but still conceptually whole. Seeking perpetually to reconnect with a lost era through literary association and symbolic referent, Jones could not have followed the positivist's version of history as a purely linear event. Like T. S. Eliot in 'Tradition and the Individual Talent', Jones's visual and literary work functions within the premise of a cyclical history in which the presence of the past and the 'pastness' of the present constantly interact.

In this respect, both Eliot and Jones were following a Continental path which sought to reject positivism in favour of re-engagement with past epochs. In the late 19th and early 20th centuries, historians such as Jacob Burckhardt had attempted to move the subject of history away from scientific, evolutionary models towards a subtler, more intuitive field. Similarly, Henri Bergson believed in the 'concordance' of past and present – that is, in the endurance of the past and the necessity of organic evolution.

It was into this new field of historical research that Oswald Spengler emerged. His hugely successful *The Decline of the West* (*Der Untergang des Abendlandes*), was published in the final year of the First World War. Its simplicity appealed to a large audience, Spengler taking a broad-ranging approach as opposed to a dryly specific reading of the past. Moreover Spengler's belief that Western civilization was in the unavoidable process of destroying itself fed into a post-war *zeitgeist*. He offered his readers an explanation for the horror they had endured, pointing out that this was not the first time such destruction had been visited on humanity by humanity and describing war as

> no longer a momentary constellation of casual facts due to national sentiments, personal influences or economic tendencies . . . but . . . a type of *a historical change of phase* occurring within a great historical organism of definable compass at the point preordained for it hundreds of years ago. [1]

Spengler saw the linear view of history as egotistical and flawed in its

---

[1] Oswald Spengler, *The Decline of the West*, ed. Helmut Werner (Oxford: OUP, 1991) 37.

assumption of ever-increasing perfection, arguing it should be rejected in favour of a cyclical (i.e. non-progressive) approach. These cycles comprise 'High Cultures'; namely, Babylonian, Indian, Chinese, Egyptian, Mexican, Arabian, Classical and West European. From birth, Spengler argued, societies move onto a 'culture phase', and from there to a 'civilisation phase'. The culture phase establishes the rituals surrounding the 'prime symbol', the semiotic cornerstone of this authentic society. The subsequent 'civilisation phase' is a period of corruption and decay where these symbols no longer function: it is marked by urbanisation, capitalism, the rise of tyranny, and the end of democracy. Eventual dictatorship leads to a return to feudal life and disillusionment with material wealth, so citizens once again search for symbols to provide meaning. Despite such ostensible defeatism, Spengler also urged people to hold out against the corruptions of decline as long as possible; asking for resistance to conserve signs and meanings of the original symbol-culture.

From the time of publication, opinion was drastically divided about the merits of Spengler's work. Academics were critical of its tendency towards gross generalisation, yet its popularity among the reading public was unrivalled. David Jones was one such enthusiast (along with Eliot and Ezra Pound), at one stage describing himself as 'saturated' in the historian's theory. Despite Jones's reservations about Spengler's style of presentation, he found the work 'enormously interesting and full of true things, astonishingly acute intuitions, and undeniable facts'. [2]

Spengler, then, provides us with a close theoretical (and acknowledged) accompaniment to Jones's ideas about historical development and continuity. As a work about cultural identities, it also gives us a foundation for reading Jones's most celebrated literary work, the prose-poem written about his experiences as a soldier in the Great War: *In Parenthesis*. In presenting a version of history which dismisses the idea of a forward-marching, progressively perfecting civilisation – *The Decline of the West* offers a basis for reading Jones's modernist play on temporality.

Jones's representation of the Great War as a re-enactment of previous conflicts is one of his primary differences as war-poet. He was consumed with the search for precedence and continuity, believing that, in the cultural deposits of Britain, one could find a pattern at work: a primordial design shaping actions and events across time.

It is obvious that Jones did not regard the Great War as an isolated, unprecedented event. As well as referring in *In Parenthesis* to many seminal war epics (including *The Iliad* and *The Aeneid*), Jones also draws on the journals of Caesar, Geoffrey of Monmouth, and others, inculcating 'real' history into his work. In addition, the literary source most closely associated with *In Parenthesis*

---

[2] David Jones, *Dai Greatcoat: A Self-Portrait of David Jones in his Letters*, ed. René Hague (London: Faber & Faber, 1980), 116.

is Aneirin's early epic *Y Gododdin*; an historically-based story of Welsh soldiers going to fight the English at Catraeth. All these factors combine to place the role of the past centre-stage, something which is additionally emphasised by Jones's use of archaic language:

> Mr Jenkins found his speech low-toned and regulated, lest he should wake the slumbering secrets of that place. A pallid Very-light climbed up from away in front. This gate of Mars armipotente . . . like flat painted scene in top lights' crude disclosing . . . With the across movement of that light's shining, showed long and strait the dark entry, where his ministrants go, by tunnelled ways, whispering. [3]

It is important to realise that Jones is not attempting to traditionalise the Great War by using such antiquated phraseology. *In Parenthesis* does not seek alternate means of eulogising the war through reverence of the 'knight-heroic' version of history. What Jones offers is a radical, and quite modern, perspective. He depicts a past which is at once sedimentary and fluid, unshakeably authoritative, yet transiently mutable in its involvement in the poetic discourse. As Jonathan Miles explains in his discourse on Spengler; 'Cyclical patterns tend towards the abolition of time . . . and free man to an extent from the terror of history'. [4] Similarly freed from the dogma of progressive time, Jones was able to depict the past as a striking presence. *In Parenthesis* is filled with the shadows of Catraeth, Agincourt, and Troy. Yet these are more than mere fragments of memory to haunt the 'real' event. Jones is not saying, 'whilst in the trenches I was reminded of a conflict long ago'. He actually revives the past; so restores the notion of history as a confluent, rather than simply continuous, event:

> Every man's speech was a perpetual showing: now of Napier's expedition, now of the Legions at the Wall, now of Jack Cade, of John Ball, of the commons in arms. [5]

Using an 'eternal now', Jones connects the threads of past, present, and future in such a way that they become almost inseparable. 'The battles [he says] are not long ago – they are today and also tomorrow'. [6]

This fits Jones's sense of a deeply scored tradition already operative along the Western Front. In one scene, as new soldiers enter the trench-system they come across a subverted folk-world ingrained within,

---

[3] David Jones, *In Parenthesis: Seinnyessit e Gledyf ym Penn Mameu* (1937; London: Faber & Faber, 1963), 44.
[4] Jonathan Miles, *Backgrounds to David Jones* (Cardiff: University of Wales Press, 1990), 39.
[5] *In Parenthesis*, Preface, xi.
[6] David Jones, *The Dying Gaul and Other Writings*, ed. Harman Grisewood (London: Faber & Faber, 1978), 127.

and sense here near habitation, a folk-life here, a people, a culture already developed, already venerable and rooted. [7]

One is immediately aware of an 'antique beginning'. In these and other passages Jones is representing a form of Spenglerian 'culture-phase' which nevertheless transcends its own epoch; a poetic version of Spengler's 'intercultural contemporaneity'. In this instant, the past and present inhabit one and the same space. The polarisation which usually occurs in Great War writing – one which either sets a barbarous presence against a departed 'golden age' or dismisses that time of ignorance in the face of sceptical, heightened knowledge – is absent from *In Parenthesis*. There is no point at which Jones objectively dissects 'ancient' and 'modern', or divides 'before' from 'after'. Instead, he styles a network of projection and recapitulation; one which knows no undiluted here-and-now:

> The last few moments came, and became the past. The last candle was snuffed out and thrust still warm at the wick and pliable into your tunic pocket. [8]

'Pliable' is the perfect description of Jones's evocation of time: a shapelessness that hardens into solid matter for only an instant – before further transmogrification. The quotation is also strikingly similar to Spengler's remark that

> every trait of the actual waking-consciousness, whether it be feeling or understanding, is in the moment of our becoming aware of it, already past. [9]

All of this mutable historicity has a powerful effect on the shape of *In Parenthesis*. Plot-wise, the action is chronological; superficially at least. The soldiers leave England for France; they are billeted before journeying to the trenches; after a period of 'alarms and excursions' they face battle. Within this particular chronology, however, there are frequent deviations from tense-form. Because of Jones's manner of interspersing dialogue devoid of quotation marks within the text, the present tense often intrudes on the past and *vice versa*:

> The more contriving had already sought out nails and hooks on which to hang their gear for the night, and to arrange, as best they might, their allotted flooring.
> They would make order, for however brief a time, and in whatever wilderness.
> Anyway, get what rest you can. I'll be along at 4.30 – yes, everything I'm afraid.
> There's talk of dumping valises – yes – we're taking them in. I think greatcoats folded – they may change that – waterproof capes worn. [10]

---

[7] *In Parenthesis*, 49.
[8] Ibid., 16.
[9] *The Decline of the West*, 89.
[10] *In Parenthesis*, 22-23.

Here are three tense forms; three different voices. One is the author, the 'old soldier' recalling those details from the past in the past tense; the second voice is less tangible: an ethereal narrative or Greek chorus speaking in the future conditional: the third voice, in the present tense, is the word of military command. Turns of phrase and shifts in perspective sharply reflect fluctuations of time. In such a fashion the mesmerising presence of 1915-16 functions 'like no-man's-land between yesterday and tomorrow'. [11] Just as chronology mutates, so does language. Archaic forms and subject matter are renewed by contemporary trench nuance:

> They'll feel the pinch alright at
> Daffy Shenkin's Great Assize.
> Roll on the Resurrection.
> Send it down David.
> Rend the middle air
> Send it down boy. [12]

Initially, such references seem at odds with the disordered, colloquial state of Jones's soldiers. Yet the everyday language of the troops actually complements the mannered ceremony of other quotes. To that end, Jones makes direct comparisons between the comradeship of ancient soldiers with that of the 'foot-mob' at the Front.

> Men marched, they kept equal step . . .
> Men marched, they had been nurtured together. [13]

If anything, Jones actually extended Spengler's theory of repeating cycles beyond the argument in *The Decline of the West*. While Spengler insisted on the idea of repeated patterns of human behaviour, he also sharply divided each of his 'High Cultures', effectively disbarring potentially useful historical and symbolic connections. Jones, by contrast, allows for much greater interaction between culture-phases (essentially the Classical and West European), so took the notion of repeated cycles to a different level by allowing for a clear line of inference between the worlds of Ancient Rome, Celtic Britain or Shakespearean England, and twentieth-century Europe. His sense of connection with the past exceeds the single millennium allotted to each 'High Culture' by Spengler. By means of artistic/literary quest and etymological inference, Jones uses the intuitive,

[11] Ibid., 181.
[12] Ibid., 18.
[13] Aneirin, 'Y Gododdin', *In Parenthesis*, epigraph to Part One.

timeless freedom of Spengler's theory to creatively blur the latter's careful segregation of epochs.

One of the clearest examples of this is Jones's use of mythology to demonstrate the repetitive nature of history. He gave much thought to the etymology and literary integration of myth (translated from Greek by him as 'a word uttered, something told').[14] As such, Jones did not regard the notion of mythology in terms of plain truth and falsehood, but rather as establishing archetypal patterns. For him, myth provides a platform for the essential kinship between cosmic forms and common expression of ordinary experience. Initiation, renaissance, sacrifice: all these are, for him, mythic patterns. Myth (or Jones's preferred *mythos*) is therefore a way of encapsulating universal experiences; of bringing metaphysical and transgressive archetypes to bear on the course of history. From this cross-bred ideology, the notion of a unified, universal story quickly emerges:

There is only one tale to tell even though the telling is patient of endless development and ingenuity and can take a million variant forms.[15]

This is not to say that the cosmology of literature is merely reiterative or stubbornly insistent; Jones is arguing as much for diversity as for uniformity; for imaginative collation within historic preservation:

To conserve, to develop, to bring together, to make significant for the present what the past holds, without dilution or any deleting, but rather by understanding and transubstantiating the material, this is the function of genuine myth, neither pedantic nor popularizing, not indifferent to scholarship, nor antiquarian, but saying always: 'of these thou hast given me have I lost none'.[16]

For Jones, artifice becomes the means of forming a text which is as permutational as history, and refractive as the intellect itself. An awareness of historical context and continuity is accordingly vital to the understanding of any act of 'making'. Jones selects from *Y Gododdin* those passages relating to companionship, to apprehension and the fear of death. He draws the sufferings of the Great War into an arena of universal warfare. In so doing, he is not attempting to negate the particular, personal tragedies of the First World War, nor to suggest an antique or fictional nature to the conflict. Rather, Jones aims to communicate a depth of loss within an omnipresent dimension, and in so doing he introduces a cosmic

[14] David Jones, *The Anathemata: Fragments of an Attempted Writing* (London: Faber & Faber, 1952), Preface,
[15] Ibid., 35.
[16] David Jones, *Epoch and Artist*, ed. Harman Grisewood (London: Faber & Faber, 1959), 243.

dimension to his exegesis. By allying the soldiers of Catraeth with those of the Western Front, he transposes the specific into the universal.

Spengler provides an appealing analytical background to *In Parenthesis*, offering an intellectual-historical context which is so often absent from discussion of Jones. Moreover, *The Decline of the West* powerfully engages with what was one of the great difficulties for Jones: the dilemma of whether one can re-engage with the past confidently, or even adequately. It was Spengler's view that some people would and *should* seek vestiges of the symbol-bound 'culture phase' even in the midst of the decline of the 'civilisation phase'. If one views Jones as just such a figure, it begins to make sense of his approach to tradition. Through a subtle re-working of earlier stories, styles, and ideas, he was able to appropriate a war (and re-appropriate an imagery) which, for many, had erased all notions of structured historical continuity. One can therefore read *In Parenthesis* as occupying the same territory of cultural cyclism offered by Spengler, the effect of which marks its radical departure from other war-verse and demonstrates strict linearity giving way to complex, time-disordered reconfigurations. As a mark of his sophistication as a poet, Jones was not only able to live with such temporal disjuncts, but to use them to extraordinary poetic effect. In this light, one can appreciate more fully what Jones does with his literary resources and historical references: he uses them to open up the possibility of a pertinent, contemporary history and to draw attention to the memorial process. Throughout, *In Parenthesis* suggests an awareness of the past which simultaneously highlights a careful recognition of historical confluence and universal loss.

Harriet Torr

The Old Soldier

Sometimes, whole universes skim across his retina
as he steps outside to put out the cat or empty the ash,
and he is struck like a blind man when the comet passes
as the one thing he is certain of calls him back into the house,
the small assurances of lounges, the asseveration of pork and chips,
the midnight silences between the TV ads. where ghost writers drift
between his polished guns and survival kit.

And sometimes, only the hammering of moths
disturbs the silence, as the old solder sits like a monk in a cell.
His thoughts have burned out on the page of his mind,
where the voyages of warships began,
the dark mountains where the river's blood is carried
down to the rocks and stones; the base lines of a valley's grief,
where echoing voices call back the dead, again and again.

But today, only his father's image is clear, not an old soldier
but a cobbler, with his eternal last straddling the kitchen floor
making the fit, smoothing the leather, ironing the crinkles,
imagining the owner of these shoes striding through
the wonder of plough-sharing fields, swallows' eggs and squirrels.
And he, an emperor of soles at the gate, watching the universe
march by, all booted and laced, all heaven shining in his face.

Sally Lucas

Poems of the Seven Chakras

Base Chakra

I am rooted in Earth,
And mould the fibres of your bones;
The colour of blood, I am a tale of rubies,
Garnet glow grounding your spine,
And gentle jasper;
I am the poppies in a field
And dark heuchera.
I am a feast of cherries by the robin's breast
And maple's autumn red.

Holding your restless feet,
I breathe you mossy odours,
Shaking your thoughts' mist,
Keeping you stable in the rush of world,
Tethered between Earth's moments,
Resting in crimson circles where you are secure.

Sacral Chakra

I am a grove of orange trees,
A bite of apricots,
Their fluid sweetening your wrists.
I gleam in golden fishy scales
And stroke your skin that loves to curve
Into cool streams.
I am your juices and your healing tears.
Discover me in orange calcite and carnelian,
Explore their light lapping your glance,
Or find me in eschscholzia, marigold and crocus
Brimming with certainty of the bright day.

I am your recognition of Spring's fecundity.
Search, search your warm waters
For the swelling seed.
Allow my creativity to flow through you,

Dripping from your fingertips,
Making, blooming,
Tasting my circles of sustenance.

Solar Plexus Chakra

Bask in my warmth
For I am fire in the wilderness.
Walk into the desert and fear nothing
For I am the sand beneath your soles.
In the cave's mouth,
Seek me in candle flame.
With a sizzle of wood, I warm your food,
Re-entering your dark tunnels.

Expand with me in a flicker of topaz,
Tiger's eye, citrine…
Dance with me in the yellow hearts of daisies
With the powdered bee,
A breeze of daffodils
Or under palest foam of ladies mantle;
Hide in a buttercup.
Laugh in a sunbeam where I turn in your vitality
And know you are strengthened
By my circles of gold.

Heart Chakra

I breathe you a wild rose blushing in the hedgerow
Or a flower of gardens.
Inhale my airiness in columbines,
Herb Robert and the shaded foxglove.
I am cool apple blossom, in its pink and green
Are correspondences of bloom and leaf,
Of linked fingers, travel between tongues.
I am the meadow breeze lifting a feather
And the messages of doves.
Feel me in silk of rose quartz
Or a shower of emeralds,
Serene in jade or green adventurine.

I am your rosy breath telling of heart's way,
How your path may turn;

Tenderly your loves are held in my green hands;
With the gentle dawn I brush your pulse;
I am your heart's wisdom:
Step lightly through my leafy circles.

Throat Chakra

I am the voice of larks calling to you,
A flash of kingfishers.
I am a whisper in the dusk
Causing a leaf to drop.
I am the palette of tropic seas and lakes.
I am meconopsis and forget-me-not
And sparkling speedwell   .
I am brilliance of turquoise and aquamarine,
A sigh of celestite.

From your expressive throat,
I am a bridge between chakras
Where words tumble and fly
In an infinity of shapes.
Hear me in soprano and bass,
A twitter of sparrows and the lion's roar
Revolving and replenishing the arcs of sound.
Listen and reply to my sky blue that appears daily
To serenade your inner ear
And open your voice to my singing circles.

Brow Chakra

Spread your thoughts along my swallows' wings,
My petals of the iris;
Fall into my deep anchusa blue,
Into my pool of sapphires,
Twilight of lapis lazuli.
I am your restful night, still as sodalite.

I am tranquil shadows of the summit snows;
Allow my farthest blue
To nourish your perceptions
For I am your gap of time,
Your knowing of another in a deep sea dream,

A crystal cave,
A gaze of cornflowers.
I cleanse your intuition with my dark falls,
Washing your inner eye,
Rolling your imagination up distant mountains.
See clearly from my circles of indigo.

Crown Chakra

I hold your rhythms in the perfumed lilac:
Trust my fragrant blooms.
I am campanula and honeyed buddleia;
My perfect poise colours the flowers of lavender
Pervading sleep's opening spaces.
Feel abundance with the damson in your palm
Or purple plum between your lips.
Watch the windfalls drop
And do not struggle with my energy
That you have always known.

Be still and feel my scent of violets
Ruffle your hair
Shading your breath to amethyst
For I am your quietness in sanctuary,
Your centre in emptiness
And here in a shady corner,
I am all the Earth and stars
Turning your spirit into smile
With other worlds lighting my circles of silence.

Boris Poplavsky

White Halo

On a grey day at the railway station,
dwarfish branches are hanging.
Souls of the dead stand at the threshold.
Time falls slowly into the garden.

Somewhere audible on the low dam
is the sound of minutes fading into dust.
The sun lies low, drops down into the mud.
The life of the woods grows sad on the mountains.

It is autumn. Beneath the sky's white halo
everything is silent, weary, and waiting.
Only the bird breathes without concern,
in those blue branches in the mists above.

Voices are drowned by the noise of water.
The shore inclines to the water.
The soul stands stock still, and then relaxes,
finally losing touch with itself completely.

The monster is freer to think here,
and no longer made to struggle in torment.
There is now no one he wishes to judge,
for the heart is at rest, and has returned to nature.

Translated by **Belinda Cooke**

The world was dark, cold, transparent,
long graduating towards winter.
It was close to them who are lonely and depressed,
direct, stern and woken from dreams.

He thought: 'Calm down, be stern,
all are unhappy, all silent, all waiting,
all work and laugh and again
doze off and drop the book on their chest.

Endless nights will soon be here,
lamps will lean low over the tables,
on a steep library bench
the beggar will hide in the corner.

It will become clear that jokingly and secretly
we are still able to forgive God for pain.
Live. Pray behind closed doors.
Read black books in the abyss'.

Freezing on empty boulevards
to talk about truth till dawn,
dying blessing the living
and writing without answer till death.

The sun sinks, it's still so hot,
autumn is in the air and the park is bare.
There the lemonades burn brightly in the little hut,
and yellow pages of newspapers are in the water.

We're still so young. Rain poured all summer,
but rowing boats rocked beyond the wet glass.
Pistols cracked in the green garden.
How swiftly, how unexpectedly the summer passed.

The blue reflected in the pane so late
and the moon rose over the factory chimney.
The soul of creation – hope for mercy –
perhaps we said farewell to you with the summer.

It's quieter, clearer like this. The prisoner at sunset
is silent in the embrasure of the high prison
and a train on the crooked viaduct whistles
in the bright shining of the autumn azure.

The coaches rock and go west.
The noise of a carousel comes from the boulevard.
He looks at the glow, does not want to cry.
How dusty, how brief is the joy of departures.

Late birds rush over the tower.
How swiftly leaves forget about the sun.
The hand opens the holy pages.
Eyes close. Pain recedes.

1930

Translated by **Richard McKane**

Boris Pasternak

Mushrooming

We trudge after mushrooms.
Road. Forest. Ditches.
Road posts
to the right and to the left.

From the wide road
we walk into the dark forest.
Our ankles in dew
we stray in all directions.

And the sun under the bushes
on *milk-agaric* and *coral milky caps*
through thickets of dark,
throws light from the edge of the forest.

The mushroom hides behind a stump,
on the stump sits a bird.
Our shadow – to us is a landmark
so we don't lose the way.

But in September the time
is measured so scantily,
that the sunset scarcely reaches us
through the thicket.

Stuffed little baskets,
topped to the brim.
More than half
are *cap mushrooms*.

We walk away. Behind our back –
the motionless forest like a wall
where the day in the beauty of the land
suddenly burned down.

1956

Translated by **Belinda Cooke**

Superstition

My little room
is a box with bitter red oranges.
No sense in muddying the mind with rooms,
count graves, till the morgue.

I came to live here for the second time
out of superstition.
The colour of the wallpaper is brown oak,
and the door sings as it creaks.

I wouldn't let the door handle out of my grip,
but you burst out,
and my forelock touched your wonderful hair,
and my lips the violets.

O my tender one, in honour
of other times and this one
your dress chirps 'Hello!'
like a snowdrop greeting April:

It's a sin to think that you're not a Vestal virgin.
You came in with a chair:
you took my life off the shelf
and blew the dust away.

Translated by **Richard McKane**

Two Chosen Broadsheet Poets

Julie Barraclough and Michael Molan

Julie Barraclough is 17 and lives in Sunderland. She was born in San Diego, California, but has lived in England all her life. She has never had any of her poetry published before, except in the school magazine of the King's School in Tynemouth, where, in her final year, she is currently studying English Literature, History and Ancient History. Her favourite writers are Kafka and Sylvia Plath. She says of poetry: 'Sometimes it is the only way in which I can justify myself without the fear of being judged. Indeed, I believe that the art of poetry should be preserved and its voice never silenced.'

A Lost Journey

i

Everywhere to go, the blackbird throws itself away.
A miniature fishnet for the sky

It will catch the world;
Harpoon blindly stabbing repeatedly by

Its own obsolete wings
Expressionless and flat and dumb: This is a surgical mystery

A naked contemplation. Where is the pessary –
  Atlas, mute and perishing,

Fingers woven into rings of air, beard
Stitched to time. We are safe indoors

With our appliances: Disgustingly white
They steal our transparency,

Make faint our fatalism. It is a dangerous peace.
I morph myself into a million Tigers.

Their teeth will be my nails, their jaws
I will spit with, spit my tongue across the sea

Like a javelin. It will scream incessantly.
The noise will be my weapon.

ii

I am alone with a thousand others. Together we are insoluble,
Multi-shaded, a dry ocean floor.

The mirror translates us incoherently: we become one extinct hearbeat
Ticking, ticking…Long-ago ancestors

Scrutinizing with their anchored souls. They threaten
Dissolution. Antithesis Hell.

iii

Hills stand frozen. They are big lumps of dirt,
The acne of the Earth.

Do we follow these cloned landmarks
Monstrously obscene

To insects' sight, like a metal band
Annihilating hymns

In a chancel?
Flat behaviour is not guaranteed.

The moon arches a muscle in response,
A half-eaten biscuit

For the night travellers
Weary in their disillusionment,

Their footprints like a row of coffins
Waiting for burial:

The clock is counting the dead. Owls hoot
Out the minutes with red beaks

Hungry for mice tails.
We have waiting long enough for this.

iv

The sun opens its eye. Smiling indecisively
Between clouds

It coverts us,
An impregnating heat

Spawned, from last night's emptiness.
The milking atmosphere.

We are utterly lost to this conceiving
Lighthouse for the sky.

v

A storm sucks me into its roots,
Lightning buried on top

And rain on top of that.
I am an unmarked identity for the

Ground; the grave bodyguard
Is puzzled and thirsty,

Anecdotes quivering themselves
Laughable

Towards midnight's
Final hour of totalitarian fame.

Each firework crying like a baby, It
Drenches us with flamboyancy for the occasion;

Scarves of ashes spew talk from our mouths,
Wine-faces

Wrapped into hysterical colours, raucous clapping.
There is no one but the sky. Our numerous

Eyes are chained until vertigo severs the spell,
    Bodies of spark overflow a fountain, and we are done.

Michael Molan is 23 and lives in London. Born in Cardiff, South Wales, he read English at Magdalen College, Oxford and completed an MPhil in Renaissance Literature at Pembroke College, Cambridge. He currently works as a television subtitler for a broadcasting company in London. These are the first poems he has ever submitted for publication.

Fragments

'The water that webs this boat
And anchors it in strange peril
Shall nourish the root of Cynan,
The urgent birdsong of our days.'

We must move on.

I cannot reckon the date;
Days have shifted past my station
In thousands, giving no sleep.
Each day twitches with a memory
And writhes on the cabin floor
Till my heel crushes it to ink.
These stained boards must make it home
Or all is lost to the tide.

Soon I shall be a sheet of rain
Laid on the ground for a circle;
Hymns, drawing the breath of the beirdd.

Penelope; in London; as a twenty-three-year-old man

Landlocked and London, I think on the sea,
Watching the Thames, godless water and riven
Jurisdictions of written words, hidden
In the plain view of my Penelope.

Brooking demands, while self-drama unfolds
In laundry hampers I keep near the stair,
I gloat in keeping the world unaware,
Trumpeting nothing as the freshness moulds.

Taking Penelope, fixing her star,
Is victory's guarantor or transcending type,

I forget; it is swept up in flight
As I yomp up the South Bank to a bar.

Landlocked and London, salt flame of the sea,
Desperate cargo of immigrant stock
Webbing his hands in the fibrous deck-rot,
        Aping the getup of Penelope.

Cristo Deposto

A church, out of the grid of light and dark
That prints Genoa's network of dens
On stone pillars raised along the sour coast.
This church stretches its blistered walls skyward,
Harvests gloom from the warm breath of tourists
Waiting in the pit for magic to spring
From the height of the cupola.
                        An alcove:
Cristo Deposto. A false declension
Flickers, belying the certain defeat
Of the collapsed limbs, eyes fixed on hell,
The weight of a thin yellow strip of halo.
Is this the weight of testimony,
A form carved with a bloody thumb squashed
Against the blade? The dumb nimbus hovering
In gallery-whispers mumbles empathy;
Not this blade.
            My glib tongue is stuck
And I trace the shafts of light that neatly
Paint the alcove in decorous misery.
The light of the door as I turn,
Unsure if I entered for shade.

Milan

In the slow twilight of that day,
An echo's gap from the scooter-buzz
Of the brave Milanese streets,
I drew sounds like apple cores
(Drab conjurer)
But I would not play for you.

The upright's old elegance
Held a battered sconce each side
Of my fixed stare.
I gave you some half measures
That scurried across the tiled floor
In a nervous invention.

The slow horror of that memory
Dogs my days with appetite.
I am often in that room,
My fingers propped on the lid,
Listening for that time-warped sound.
But the box is all empty filth,
A dead mechanism of hope.
The rusting strings eat themselves
To the red of the lidded sky.
Before waking, not Milan.

Notes for Broadsheet Poets 9

It is heartwarming for budding and struggling young poets to note that quite a few **Broadsheet poets** go on to have noteworthy collections published. Examples of these have been Catriona O'Reilly, Steven O'Brien, Will Stone, Sasha Dugdale, P. Viktor, Kathryn Gray, and Leanne O'Sullivan. Now, hot off the press, are three more: **Zoe Brigley**'s *The Secret*, a Poetry Book Society Recommendation (Bloodaxe, £8.95), **Tupa Snyder**'s *No Man's Land* (Shearsman Books, £8.95) and **Adam O'Riordan**'s pamphlet, *queen of the cotton cities* (tall-lighthouse pilot publications, £4).

All three are highly impressive, with assured voices that seem mature beyond their years, if years are relevant at all in terms of poetic talent.

Zoe Brigley, who is Welsh and only 26, covers not only a complex range of worlds in her collection but also plays with language excitingly and refreshingly. She says of her book that it 'emerges from silence and the secrets'. The first of the three sections cleverly reconciles Tarot symbols with modern life. The second section, 'The Greater Secrets', uses the structure of a twenty day cycle in the Aztec calendar, each day being characterised by a symbol, such as the lizard, snake or eagle The final sequence, 'The Curse of the Long-tailed Bird', explores Mexican mythologies and Western fairytales. There are so many archetypes, so much cosmic myth, and such very clever play with knitting the Welsh language into English and vice versa that the reader is almost overwhelmed at such brilliance. Her collection leaves one breathless at her ingenuity, her music, her erudition, and originality. She is a very serious and daring poet with huge scope and someone definitely to watch.

Tupa Snyder has a very different voice and a very compelling one also. Her poems are perhaps more immediately accessible, and she, too, tackles different layers and levels of meaning with an acute intelligence, illuminating, like Zoe Brigley, a vast world. Tupa grew up in India, a child of the remnants of the Raj, and the British Enpire. Here she shifts her inscapes, landscapes and musical lyrics between the decadent world of the Raj, the new U.S. world, the mid-world of England and the new India plagued by the persistence of the old. Her colourful, vibrant images bring India to life and her smooth, beautifully handled transitions from one place, topic or person to another, her use of repetition and interwoven images are reminiscent of Virgina Woolf in 'Mrs. Dalloway'. Her mesmeric, philosophical poems about fragmentation, identity, family, nation, the self, memory, place and language, reveal a unique vision of the Anglo-Indian heritage. Again, she is someone to take note of.

Adam O'Riordan's pamphlet *queen of the cotton cities* is equally awesome and shows an incisive active mind at work crafting language with music and concision. Like the two ladies above, he has a broad vision. In these beautifully honed poems, not a word seems out of place, and he demonstrates a broad grasp of history, philosophy, religions, myth, even cosmology and physics – while remaining a young poet very much of this time. On the last page of this pamphlet, the reader is left looking for more. His next, full collection is surely worth waiting for.

This pilot series of pamphlets published in the tall-lighthouse pilot series marks an exciting and very worthwhile new initiative to introduce to a new audience some of the best young poets under 30 writing in Britain today, under the editorial guidance of Roddy Lumsden. 18 pamphlets over a period of three years are planned and the launch of Adam's pamphlet, along with another, Abi Curtis's humbug, marked the launch of the series in May of this year.

Another first collection by a young poet still in her twenties worthy of note is **Elizabeth Whyman**'s *Touchpiece*, published by the poetry can, hot off the press at £8. Original, fresh, well-crafted, energetic and very much of our day, yet with a subtle intelligence pushing them forward into a lived-in wisdom, these poems are both pleasing in their aliveness, yet unsettling at the same time. U.A. Fanthorpe says, 'Psychiatrist, detective and photographer meet in this striking new collection'. Elizabeth has not yet submitted any of her work to the **Agenda Broadsheets** as yet, but it is hoped that she will submit some new poems soon.

Of course, it must be remembered that not all young poets will get their work published when they are young. There is a right time for everything, and for some people, a lifetime's wait might be required – or even a wait until after death! Poets must not be deflated regarding the publishing market. In every age there are some good poets who do not get published, and, perhaps in our age, too many who do. After all, what matters is the quality of the poetry that is being written. No matter what, poets should keep on writing, persevering, learning the craft, listening to the muse, scribbling down the poems that are pressed out of them, even if these only come in snatches. The main focus should not be on becoming a commercial salesperson for a sheaf of poems, but on achieving the poem that is envisaged in the head and heart. As **Seamus Heaney** said in a letter to *Agenda*, 'Hush. No fuss. And proceed'.

*   *   *   *

The following extract from a longer interview between the well-known poet and essayist, **Peter Robinson**, a regular contributor to *Agenda*, and **Belinda Cooke** whose fine translations have appeared in *Agenda* and feature in this issue serves to inspire as **Notes for Broadsheet Poets 9**. The full interview is available online www.agendapoetry.co.uk

from Peter Robinson in conversation with Belinda Cooke

So if you do get asked, how do you see yourself fitting into the contemporary poetry scene? And what is your take on what's currently happening in poetry?

A friend of mine once said that poets' positions in the scene (if there is one) are created by a kind of vacuum forming. You're sucked into the only space that is available for you – if at all. If that is the case, then there are reasons for fearing the shape that you'll end up being deformed into, and of keeping on doing whatever you do in despite it all. It's rather that writing for me is an activity fed by going about in ordinary life and feeding my obsessions with poetry, past and present, alongside related matters. The scene, then, is the situation in which you find your work read or ignored, appreciated or criticized, whether you like it or not. A lot of activity recently has been about trying to persuade people to buy poetry books in numbers but the signs are they won't. If you pay much attention to the book-sales' agenda you won't be concentrating on the likely sources of your art. Communicating with actual or imagined readers in the form of interlocutors for the poetry you write is a significantly different matter: poems can be successful, communicative works of art in that sense without adding to sales at all. You ask what's going on at the moment. The poets of the fifties are thinning out to extinction; the sixties' vanguard and others are now the grand old figures. Then there are the lost generations and the few 'representative' types picked out to stand for what is supposed to be happening now – some of them getting pretty long in the tooth and weighed down with awards. At least two new generations of writers have come up in the almost two decades that I've been away in Japan. My hunch would be that representative factionalizing by which poets are recruited for sales identity purposes to represent national, ethnic, gender, sexual orientation, or generational sub groups has not yet run its course, tired though it may be looking. There's nothing convincing in the way of new movements. Some from the later generations of the sixties vanguards are still claiming special status. It's business as usual, I suppose.

You've put it in a nutshell there. One thinks of Pasternak's 'It's not good to be famous': 'The goal of art – is to give yourself, /not to create a stir, or be an overnight success. /It's a disgrace knowing nothing, /to be a name on everyone's lips.' What convinces you that a poem of yours has become 'successful'? Are you your own critic or do you have close poet friends you depend on (à la Robert Lowell and Elizabeth Bishop for example)?

Well, I didn't mean to make unqualified claims for anything I've written. People, not usually poets, do sometimes tell you, though. Miki Iwata, who wrote one of the essays in *The Salt Companion* on my work, and has translated some of the poems into Japanese (well, I'm told), she has said she likes 'Pasta-Making', a poem whose interlocutor helped to translate it into Italian. Someone else tells me their favourite is 'The Coat Hanger', and that one prompted some eloquent words from Roy Fisher in the Preface to the *Companion*. You can experience instances where a poem seems to have succeeded for you, and others tell you they like it, so you feel a more or less unalloyed satisfaction – without that impacting on royalty statements.

Well, maybe, but having benefited from the explosion in creative writing courses of the past 20 years with your new post, I'd like to hear your thoughts on creative writing courses. Do you think anyone can become a poet?

It's true I've been asked to launch a module and head creative writing at Reading; but mine's a chair in English and American literature – and creative writing is not why they employed me, I don't think (it's because there are books of criticism and translation with academic presses in the UK and the States). Doubtless being fairly *persona grata* here after all these years has been helped by the fact that poets are no longer so anathematized in the groves of British academe. What do I think about creative writing? In the scale of man's inhumanity to man it's fairly harmless! It probably comes in there with homeopathic medicine: not likely to do much damage, it may even do some good. Can anyone become a poet? Certainly they can. No one is *born* a poet. Art is a way of life. It's an interwoven set of cultural practices that have to be entered and learned in order for someone to contribute usefully to advancing them. What it involves is commitment and study, plus the good fortune to have a developed aptitude for words and a linguistic background that appreciates inventive usage. A reasonably cultivated taste for the other arts helps too, especially music and painting. I don't think it's useful to think of poetry as produced by those who were destined from birth to be poets; rather, it is made by people who have found they need to devote themselves obsessively to this activity – and in a culture where there are creative writing courses, well, they might help such souls find their way. One of the best must be Bill Manhire's at the University of Victoria in Wellington. A great many of the contemporary writers in New Zealand have gone through there.

I've never quite got out of my system Osip Mandelstam's belief that one is only a poet if acknowledged to be so by another poet: what he termed 'recognition'. He limited his own inner circle to about four other poets.

Me too, I internalized that in the 70s. The word 'poet' is an honorific: other people have to attribute you with the condition of being one. What we do is try to write the best poetry that we're able and hope that others find it so.

But I do think there are too many poems produced as a result of writing exercises picked up from self-help books or one-day courses. My pet hate is the obsessive use of dramatic monologues: 'Today let's pretend to be Eva Braun. Now what was she thinking in that bunker?'

Oh I don't know ... Perhaps I should encourage students to write dramatic monologues pretending to be themselves; but, seriously, the dramatic monologue problem comes from the widespread view, heard from the amateur poet guidebook to the avant-garde manifesto, that we should avoid the first-person singular. My view is that we should use that pronoun as a way of accessing significant experience. It's the one way I know to escape from the twin imperatives that will reduce subject-matter to zero at a stroke: namely, you mustn't write about other people's experience because it's appropriative and presumptuous (unfair to Eva Braun), and, equally, you mustn't write about your own experience because it's vain, selfish, egocentric, not to say, solipsistic – a word I've had hurled at my head in the past. Others embrace loss of subject matter and write about language itself; but, frankly, that's been done to death in the last century, and, anyway, all good poems are simultaneously about both their own and the language.

Speaking as one who has sweated eight and half years completing a PhD part-time while holding down a full time teaching post I recall it as an experience of permanent insecurity as to whether it's achievable, years before the writing is even nearing the right quality and above all reading lots of books – a labour of love, of course, but it leaves me wondering what are these creative writing PhDs?

I don't yet know anything about them. My module is for second-years, and we also offer the possibility of students offering a finals dissertation in creative writing. There is nothing available yet beyond that at Reading, as far as I know. However, even with these two options, we require students to submit essays on the relationship between their creative writing and inspirational or sponsoring works from the body of the literature we study and teach in the department. I'm in favour of this because the sense of art as a form of life sketched above also means that you like reading very large amounts of work by your elders, contemporaries, or juniors. So the study and enjoyment of literature and the making of it are all part of the same commitment.

Ezra Pound suggested a twenty-year tutelage, which seems only fair since you'd need the same for music or painting – which leads nicely into the place of translation as part of that study. You'd surely agree about that?

It's invaluable if you're drawn to it. A student at Notre Dame asked me after a reading from the Sereni book that came out in 2006 what gains I had from translating poetry for my own writing. What I didn't think of in time, and regret not being quick enough to say, was this: translation, done properly, teaches you to be respectful of your own material. There's a connection, that's to say, between being 'reckless with literal meaning' as Lowell admits in his Introduction to *Imitations* and the recklessness with his own meanings that cruelly mars the later volumes. I've mentioned somewhere in *Talk about Poetry* a feeling of nausea that would come while belabouring a piece of my own, desperately trying to 'make it work as a poem'. Translating is a way of learning techniques and, simultaneously, respect for others' techniques for meaning. If the translation doesn't come off, you haven't squandered an irreplaceable occasion of your own. You can either revise or abandon without intimate loss. If you spoil a poem of your own there can be inner recriminations and despair. So the lesson is: you learn respect for yourself, your own life and work, by practising it in the translation of others' works.

Biographies

William Bedford first appeared in *Agenda* in 1972. He has published novels, children's fiction and poetry around the world. His novel *Happiland* was short-listed for the *Guardian* Fiction Prize. He has received major awards from The Arts Council, The Society of Authors and The Royal Literary Fund.

Alison Brackenbury's latest collection is *Bricks and Ballads* (Carcanet, 2004). New poems can be seen on her website, www.alisonbrackenbury.co.uk

Marianne Burton's pamphlet *The Devil's Cut* (Smiths Knoll) is the Poetry Book Society's 2007 summer pamphlet choice.

Sally Carr is a prize-winning poet and her poems have appeared widely in magazines. She has published two collections: *Electrons on Bonfire Night*, 1997, and *Handing on the Genes*, 2003, both from Rockingham Press. A third collection is near completion. She lives in Wiltshire.

Annie Charlesworth has only recently come out of hibernation in the depths of Devon where she writes poetry and paints.

Belinda Cooke was born in Reading in 1957. She completed her doctorate on Robert Lowell in 1993. Her poetry, translations, articles and reviews have been published widely. She has published one chapbook *Resting Place* (Flarestack in 2007) and *Paths of the Beggarwoman: the Selected Poems of Marina Tsvetaeva* is forthcoming with Worple Press (spring 2008). She teaches in Scotland.

David Cooke was born in Cheshire. He graduated in English from London University and worked for a number of years for the Poetry Library in London. His poems have appeared in numerous poetry magazines including *Poetry Wales, Orbis, Stand* and *Babel*.

Darius Degher, the grandson of immigrants from Italy and Lebanon, was born and raised in Southern California. He has a BA in English from UCLA and an MA in creative writing from Lancaster University. As a writer of poetry, he says he's interested in 'finding the song in each poem' and that he 'respects both language and subject.' He teaches writing and literature at Malmo University in southern Sweden, where he lives with his wife and two daughters. He is also a songwriter and musician.

Martin Dodsworth taught English at Royal Holloway, University of London, for many years. He was associated with *the review*, and reviewed poetry in *The Guardian* for almost twenty years. He edited *The Survival of Poetry* (1970)

Tim Dooley's most recent collection *Tenderness* (2004) was a winner in the Poetry Business pamphlet competition and a Poetry Book Society pamphlet choice. His new book-length collection *Keeping Time* is due from Salt next spring.

Kate Edwards completed her PhD thesis, entitled 'Beyond Englishness: Culture and Context in Relation to David Jones's *In Parenthesis*', in 2005 at the University of Kent. She now teaches part time at the Centre for Continuing Education at the University of Sussex and is currently writing a book on the Jewish population of central Italy during the Renaissance.

Lenny Emmanuel's first collection, *The Icecream Lady*, was published in 1997 (Ramparts, Inc. and Indiana University). He has published internationally in leading literary and scientific magazines in Australia, Canada, India, England, and the U.S. In 1998 he became poetry and contributing editor of *The New Laurel Review*.

Marc Harris was born in 1962 in Cardiff. He spent 30 years living in England but returned to Wales in 2000 and now works with homeless people in Cardiff. His poems, which have won prizes, have been widely published in the UK, Ireland, the U.S. and New Zealand.

Stephen Knauth's latest collections are *The River I Know You By* and *Twenty Shadows*, both from Four Way Books. His poems have appeared in *North American Review, Virginia Quarterly Review, New Orleans Review*, and *Poetry Daily*. He has received two creative writing fellowships from the National Endowment for the Arts. He lives in North Carolina.

Mark Leech's sequence *London Water* will be published by Flarestack in 2007. He won the Stephen Spender prize for poetry in translation in 2004, and has had poems and translations published in a wide range of magazines. He lives in Oxford.

Sally Lucas has had poems published in various magazines and has appeared in a few anthologies.

Richard McKane was born in Melbourne of British parents in 1947. An Oxford graduate, he is the translator from Russian and Turkish of over twenty books of poetry. Three collections of his own poetry have been published. He has worked as an interpreter at the Medical Foundation for the Care of Victims of Torture in London. He translated jointly, with Ruth Christie, *Poems of Oktay Rifat* (Anvil Press, 2007, £11.95). This book will be reviewed in *Agenda* shortly.

Sam Milne lives and works in Surrey, although his heart resides in Aberdeen. He is currently writing a long essay on the Scots dialect-writer Flora Garry who writes in Broad Buchan, his own native language. He has just written a novel which is looking for a publisher, and has completed a study on Marcel Proust which will be included in his forthcoming book of collected essays. He is also updating his critical study on the poetry of Geoffrey Hill.

Boris Poplavsky was born in Moscow in 1903 but settled in Paris after the Revolution. He belongs to a younger generation of the first emigration of Russian poets. He was regarded as one of the most talented of these younger poets when his life was tragically cut short in 1935. A fellow drug addict intent on suicide managed to poison both himself and Poplavsky. During his life he published only one book, *Flags*, but he had several posthumous collections. He also completed one novel, *Apollo Unformed*, and started another, along with writing extensive journals.
Further translations of Poplavsky can be viewed on www.agendapoetry.co.uk

Peter Robinson has recently resettled in Reading, Berkshire, where he teaches English literature at the University. He published *Talk about Poetry: Conversations on the Art* with Shearsman Books in 2006, and a new collection, *The Look of Goodbye: Poems 2001-2006* will be available from the same press in early 2008. *The Salt Companion to Peter Robinson*, a collection of critical essays on his work edited by Adam Piette and Katy Price, appeared in spring 2007.

Linda Saunders's first full-length book of poems, *Ways of Returning* (Arrowhead Press), was shortlisted last year for the Jerwood Aldeburgh First Collection Prize. Her poetry has been widely published in magazines and anthologies, including *New Women Poets* (Bloodaxe), and a chapbook, *She River*, from Vane Women Press.

Robert Sheppard, poet and critic, was educated at the University of East Anglia. He was active in the alternative poetry scene in London during the '80s and '90s before moving to Liverpool to take up a post teaching English and Creative Writing at Edge Hill University where he is currently Professor of Poetry and Poetics.

Alexander Small comes from Strathaven (Stra`ven) in Lanarkshire, Scotland, and is a graduate of Edinburgh University, with Honours in English Language and Literature. He now lives in Orkney, where he works at one of its neolithic sites. Although he has been writing for some years, his work has appeared in only a few poetry magazines.

Harriet Torr lives on a croft in the far north of Scotland, about 6 miles from Dunreay Nuclear Power Station, and she rides a mountain bike. Her poems have appeared in several magazines and anthologies in the U.K., including *Poetry News* (Poetry Society Newsletter), Arvon and Daily Telegraph prize-winners' anthology, and she was a semi-finalist in the Dorset Prize (U.S.) 2006 for her unpublished collection *The thinking man's fish*. A poem is forthcoming in *Stand*.

Andrew Waterman was born in London in 1940. After various clerical and manual jobs, he read English literature at Leicester University, and from 1968 to 1997 taught at the University of Ulster. He now lives in Norwich. His nine books of poetry include *Collected Poems* (2000) and most recently *The Captain's Swallow* (2007), both published by Carcanet. He is a recipient of the Cholmondeley Award for Poets.His website is at www.andrewwaterman.co.uk